ARMENIAN WOMEN IN A CHANGING WORLD

Papers presented at the
First International Conference of the
Armenian International Women's Association

SEPTEMBER 19-21, 1994
CHURCH HOUSE CONFERENCE CENTER
LONDON, ENGLAND

EDITED BY
Barbara J. Merguerian
Doris D. Jafferian

AIWA Press
Armenian International Women's Association
Belmont, Massachusetts

©1995 by the Armenian International Women's Association
Post Office Box 654, Belmont, Massachusetts 02178

Library of Congress Catalog Card Number 95-83604

ISBN: 0-9648787-0-4

CONTENTS

COMMITTED BELIEVER IN THE POWER
AND POTENTIAL OF ARMENIAN
WOMANHOOD

THIS BOOK IS DEDICATED
TO THE MEMORY OF

AGNES KEOSAIAN MISSIRIAN, PhD

Businesswoman, Educator, Activist

AIWA Board Member, 1990 to 1991 and 1993 to 1994

Chair of the First International Conference
September 19-21, 1994, London, England

*"An intelligent,
motivated person can do
anything"*

Preface

We are proud to present here the compilation of papers presented at AIWA's First International Conference held in London, England, on September 19 to 21, 1994.

The book is dedicated to the memory of our dear Board Member and Conference Chair, Dr. Agnes K. Missirian. Agnes was committed to a permanent record of the proceedings of the Conference, and prior to her passing, she insured the funding for this publication.

Agnes believed that women, particularly Armenian women, as a group could move the world. She realized that the first time Armenian women around the world came together would be momentous, and with over 200 women attending, it certainly was. Numerous attenders have spoken of the enthusiasm and the sense of a new beginning that was felt in London.

Agnes inspired Armenian women internationally to contribute time and resources to insure that the Conference would succeed. Many of you reading this were moved to contribute to the work of organizing the Conference. As we know, Agnes was too ill to attend the remarkable event itself.

The thirty-two papers in this book attest to Agnes's vision and commitment. They are organized in the order of the Conference program. Much effort was made to include every presentation, but not every presenter submitted her paper. Nevertheless, we believe you will find the papers stimulating to read. For those of you who attended the Conference, we know you will be able to relive the excitement generated that week. For those of you who were unable to be present, we believe you will find the papers a fascinating historical record of Armenian women during a particular moment in time.

Enjoy!

—*Doris D. Jafferian, Ed.D.*

Introduction

The establishment in 1991 of an independent Armenian Republic in Transcaucasia in a small eastern part of the traditional Armenian homeland, following seven decades of Soviet rule and more than eight centuries of foreign domination, has opened wide and attractive vistas to the Armenians both in the homeland and in diaspora.

AIWA's first international conference took place on the third anniversary of that independence, at a time when the Armenian people were stimulated by the challenges of building a new society, yet at the same time apprehensive lest massive change destroy the distinctive characteristics of an ancient culture that survived against tremendous odds for three millennia.

If, indeed, Armenian women stand at the "dawn of a new era," as First Lady Ludmila Ter Petrossian asserts in her essay which opens this collection, it is equally clear that we today are "in the process of inventing a new kind of Armenian woman," as anthropologist Mary Catherine Bateson points out the next essay. This prospect is both exhilarating and inspiring on the one hand, and at the same time bewildering and frightening on the other.

The papers which follow attest to the vitality of Armenian women, the multiplicity of our interests, and the diversity of our backgrounds, education, and training. Yet there is a common thread that unites the authors of these papers: a confidence that is based on the past contributions Armenian women have made to our society and culture, and at the same time a frustration that Armenian women are held back, for a number of reasons, from participating fully in the political, social, and economic life of our communities and nation. This frustration is two-fold: first because the Armenian woman is thereby denied personal self-fulfillment and second because she is prevented from making her full contribution to the society in which she lives. This is as clear in the reports of the politically active women in Armenia as in the essays of the Armenian-American feminists.

It is not surprising to find the papers of the women of Armenia* dominated by concerns over the very real problems faced by the society: a struggle for existence in a nation cut off from the outside world by a longstanding blockade, which has resulted in serious shortages of the basic essentials of life, as well as by a steady drop in the standard of living as the result of the economic collapse following the fall of the Soviet Union. National survival has to be a primary focus for these women. Unfortunately, for a number of reasons, the effect of these catastrophic events has been to exclude women from decision-making at the very time that the society needs the full participation of all its citizens.

The papers of the women of the diaspora, while reflecting concern about the homeland, raise many questions dealing with the survival of a culture and a way of life in societies far removed, both geographically and psychologically, from their place of origin.

While the authors represented in this collection provide insights into the past experiences and present perspectives of Armenian women, they do no more than scratch the surface of the Armenian woman's story. Many subjects are almost entirely absent (women in the arts, women in religion); research into the history of Armenian women is an initial stage (and is reflected in widely varying interpretations); and some parts of the diaspora are presented in a cursory manner or not at all. If this volume provides a stimulus for further research, a target for analysis and discussion, and an opportunity for Armenian women to consider seriously their roles in society, both individually and collectively, it will have achieved its purpose. —*Barbara J. Merguerian, Ph.D.*

---

* Thanks to a travel grant to AIWA from the John D. and Catherine T. MacArthur Foundation, twenty women from Armenia were able to attend the Conference.

Armenian Women in a Changing World

Lucia Ter Petrossian*

It is difficult to imagine that, as recently as six years ago, the notion of a conference on "Armenian Women in a Changing World" would have been devoid of any relevance for the average Armenian woman in Yerevan, Beirut, Los Angeles, or Stepanakert. Today it is different. Until six years ago every Armenian woman born in the twentieth century was convinced that the 1915 genocide had finally exhausted the long line of tragic events suffered by the Armenians. Time had then stopped. It had stopped for almost a century.

Then the calendar turned to 1988, and in the smallest, most distant capital of the Soviet Union, people took to the streets. They did so to demand change, from slavery to freedom, from genocide to human rights, from totalitarianism to democracy. In the diaspora tens of thousands of Armenians held their breaths and followed their brothers and sisters in the homeland. Was not such heroism tantamount to madness? Would all this not end in yet another, maybe final, tragedy?

When on March 2, 1992, the flag of independent Armenia was hoisted at the United Nations headquarters in New York, joining the flags of free nations, every Armenian drew a deep, comforting breath. It was the dawn of a new era for

---

Lucia Ter Petrossian is the First Lady of Armenia. Her address to the Conference was read by Nuné Sarkissian, art historian and wife of the Armenian Ambassador to Great Britain.

the Armenian nation, a nation which had lost its independence six hundred years earlier and had suffered the worst national disaster almost a century ago. Historians of the twenty-first century will probably refer to this as the era of rebirth.

Yet again, as she has done throughout the history of the Armenian people, the Armenian woman is manifesting her bewildering vitality and her psychological resilience to global changes invading her life. While she remains the protector of the family—the traditional unit of her people's life—the woman in the new Armenia is playing an increasingly active role in the making of the state and in society in general. There are at present twenty-three women's organizations registered in Armenia, covering all aspects of public and social life and maintaining relations with their international counterparts.

Of course it would be erroneous to insist that the Armenian woman is playing a social or political role commensurate with her potential. But the process is evolving constantly and changes are already evident.

The situation in the diaspora is also changing. What I have seen in the past three years testifies to the transition from the concern for problems within the narrow boundaries of the ethnic community to issues of relevance to the international community.

The absence of her own state on the world map was, willingly or subconsciously, compelling the Armenian woman to respect artificial boundaries to her action, limited to her family and the community where she happened to live. The loss of her historic homeland, once part of historic Armenia, had engendered in her the fear of a loss of her roots as well.

I believe that the birth of the Armenian state, whose essential function entails the preservation of the national language, traditions, and culture—as it is with all other States—has given Armenian women the freedom to realize their creative and intellectual potential fully and more precisely.

The London Conference, which has for the first time brought together women with the most varied views and specializations, women representing the most diverse special and social interests, constitutes that inspiring example of the change which is taking place in the world and in the lives of Armenian women today.

Commitment in a Time of Change

Mary Catherine Bateson*

Please excuse me for speaking in English today, because I fear that if I speak in Armenian, one-third will be Western Armenian, which the Eastern Armenians call Turkish jargon, one-third will be Eastern Armenian—more or less, and the final third wrong (in Armenian).

I thought I would begin with a story of the occasion on which I first met my in-laws. To go a little further back, when I first met my husband, I went and looked up "Armenia" in the encyclopedia. But by the time we married and headed for Beirut, I had done quite a lot of studying and spoke a considerable amount of Armenian. So I arrived in Beirut, and met my husband's family, who were very sophisticated, educated people—like so many Armenians. They spoke four or five languages each—they spoke English to me. And I made a big effort to speak Armenian to them.

This went on for several days. Finally, one day we were at my in-laws house and my mother-in-law was preparing to make a dish that the Western Armenians cherish called *chekufteh*, and it happens to be a dish that symbolizes certain things about family. You wouldn't want to have it made by a stranger, and it's one of those dishes that sometimes ten years after marriage husbands go home to eat their mother's

---

*Mary Catherine Bateson is Clarence J. Robinson Professor in Anthropology and English at George Mason University and the author of several books.

version because their wife's *che-kufteh* doesn't taste quite the same. I had learned some cooking as well as learning some language, and in my frustration I walked into the kitchen and said in Armenian, "I will do that." Now here is the interesting thing. It was actually very presumptuous behavior, but from that moment on when I spoke Armenian they answered in Armenian. Looking at me they couldn't believe I spoke Armenian, whatever their ears told them. But their mouths told them that perhaps I could speak it.

There's a moral to that story. There are many different kinds of unity and mutual recognition—it's no simple matter. We've already had comments on the extraordinary diversity in this room. One of the challenges that faces Armenians today is to obtain and maintain all the benefit of the diversity of Armenian experience. The fact is that there are Armenians who know virtually every major language on the planet, who live in every major city, who together assemble a unique knowledge of the world, and who maintain that diversity with a conviction of unity. When I first heard that there were two major literary dialects of Armenian, I asked, "Can people understand each other, are they mutual intelligent, mutually intelligible?" And someone said something to me that I remembered a long time. She said, "If you want to understand each other you can, but if you don't want to understand each other it can be a problem."

I used the example of a dish that is essentially Western Armenian, but I used it to suggest something to you about family, something about the relationship between generations and how a *harse* (bride) comes into a family, that has a broader application. We have these two different elements of unity and diversity, of mutual recognition and an extraordinary opportunity to learn new things from each other.

The kitchen has been an important place for Armenians, an important part of Armenian identity and a symbol of family because, as in many traditions, Armenian women have often been in charge of continuity. Men go out and do all sorts of exciting things and change the world, and women stay home and hold it together. Women pass on tradition, they keep the home fires burning, they sit with children and tell them stories of the past, and correspond with relatives in other countries. This has been one aspect of women's traditional role—to be guardians of tradition. It has often freed men up for exploration and going to new places. The difficulty is that this particular division of labor isn't going to work in the future and is really based on a kind of illusion, because in fact if you look at traditional women's roles and traditional women's work, women have been conspicuous for their adaptability, for their capacity to change.

If, for instance, as sometimes happens, one political party announces it is conservative and the other party announces that it's the party of change, both are speaking nonsense! For our time, we need a new understanding of the relationship between continuity and change, one that does not separate them.

We can get this new understanding from, for instance, the theory of evolution: that it is only by adapting, by changing and accepting new circumstances, that a species can survive and continue to exist. When people talk about the extraordinary survival of the Armenian nation, of this very long history that is the basis of Armenian identity, it must at the same time be telling a story of constant change and adaptation, otherwise there wouldn't be Armenians anymore. Survival is possible only because of change, and the groups that disappeared are the ones that could not change.

There is a temptation at this time of the establishment of an independent Republic of Armenia to try to become like every other nation. On the other hand, there is a temptation to resist change and adaptation, to go back to one or another tradition of the past and say we must maintain this because it is fundamental to Armenian identity.

This is an important matter for women. On the one hand, the men in our lives may sometimes want us to behave in very traditional ways, to prepare this or that dish the way their mothers did, to carry on the patterns of a previous generation and "respect them" in an old-fashioned way. But on the other hand, it's essential today to recognize that the leadership roles that women will play will depend on their capacity to adapt, and perhaps their capacity to adapt in different ways from the ways that men adapt. We are all people in transition. I have made a certain transition from the family I grew up in to learning about my husband's Armenian identity, but because my parents were anthropologists, there was an odd sort of similarity between what Armenians grow up knowing and what I grew up knowing. I was raised by my parents always to know that people of different groups do things differently. My mother used to tell me, "Don't say 'This is a glass,' say 'We call this a glass,' because other people, other nationalities, call it something different." I have to say that in my time a lot of Americans didn't grow up with that point of view. Their view was, "This is a glass, and if you call it something else that's a funny foreign word you'd better forget it."

I grew up taking for granted that if you know that on the one hand it's a glass and on the other hand it's a *kavat,* and dozens of other things, you also know that without a deep and profound sense of human diversity you are not free to change and you cannot know the alternatives that exist for the future. It's very important to look at a particular institution, a particular custom, and to be able to say it doesn't have to be this way. We can change it! We can modify it! We can invent new institutions and make choices about what elements will be preserved and what elements will be modified through time. My mother used to say, when she was discussing some problem in American society, "Well, we're going to have to make a social invention." This is what the building of a new nation-state is about. It's about choosing things from the past to preserve and taking those things as the base for inventing something new. Today you are in the process of inventing a new kind of Armenian woman, a new version of this ancient identity that has been preserved for such a very long time.

Now sometimes when I talk about cultural difference, about the willingness to go and learn a new language, learn new customs, conform with the way things happen in another place, people say to me, "But let's face it, what are the fundamental commitments?"

I have to tell you another story about my wedding trip. As I started learning about my husband's culture, one of the things that I had been told is that when you are offered food you should say "no, thank you," and only the third time it is offered should you accept. Unfortunately, my husband's family knew that Americans don't have very good manners and so if they want something they will accept it the first time. You could imagine that I became rather hungry for the first few days because I kept politely saying no and was never offered a second chance. I was changing myself and they were changing themselves to establish communication, but what was underneath this adaptation that flipped us in opposite directions was a profound goodwill and an effort to bridge our differences. That was the more basic element, more fundamental than any particular custom might have been.

One of the things that occurred to me recently about women and commitment, that makes it clear that a commitment is not something fixed that you hold onto but something developmental, is the extraordinary character of the commitment that a mother has to a child.

The commitment of a mother, and ideally a father, to a child is extraordinarily fluid. Here is this being who is different from day to day, who is almost unintelligible—you know, it isn't just a newborn baby that is unintelligible and can't have a conversation, a seven-year old is unintelligible. There's always something going on in a child's mind that a grown-up doesn't understand. You're constantly trying to find a way to communicate; questions come up and you struggle for a way to phrase the answer that will make sense to this other mind which is different. Then that seven or eight-year old becomes an adolescent, and you know that half the time you still don't understand each other. It turns out that the human condition always involves change and there is never perfect understanding, so that in order to maintain a commitment it must be fluid.

The same thing is true of marriage. Males and females often don't understand each other, because they have quite different styles of communication. In addition, they change over time, so that one can't expect a spouse to stay the same. Without an openness to change, the marriage will not be viable. And children are even more profoundly strangers, whom we see changing from day to day, year to year, so that in loving a child we are making a commitment to an unknown future. We cannot say what this beloved other is going to become. The commitment transcends the changes that lie ahead.

I believe the same thing is true of a nation: the commitment involves an acceptance of change. Women have in their own experience the metaphor to understand and to resist the various kinds of dogmatism that insist on perpetuating old ideas, old prejudices, that reject the potential for change and development.

The Armenian people have survived by hanging on to a few things and changing a great many things, and by learning constantly and reaching out. Today we are talking about a new nation, a new republic, but at the same time a curiously worldwide people. My parents raised me to be a citizen of the world. I believe that all Armenians are potentially citizens of the world, for you can think in terms of being part of all humanity only if you are rooted, anchored somewhere.

I open my most recent book *Peripheral Visions* about understanding cultures and cultural diversity with a quote, "Until you are at home somewhere, you can't be at home everywhere."

This is where we are, somewhere and everywhere. This is what building bridges means. It means treasuring all the diversity in this world. It means treasuring the changes and surprises that lie ahead because of a sense of identity that transcends them, that has in the past empowered the Armenian people to adapt in a very powerful way and to live in a sense of a long long past and a long long future.

Participating in the Political Process in Iran

Emma Aghayan*

My presentation deals with my experiences as an Armenian member of the last pre-Revolutionary Parliament in Iran. However, in order to put my political life in its proper context, I would like to take a short moment to explain the recent history of Iran, and how Armenians came to be an integral part of Iranian society.

HISTORICAL BACKGROUND

Until the early nineteenth century, much of the Caucasus, including the Khanat of Yerevan, was under Persian domination. These territories were highly populated with Armenians, who considered themselves as living in their historical homeland.

The Persians lost control over much of the Caucasus, including the Khanat, to the Russian Empire in various wars which ended with the Treaty of Turkmanchai of 1828. This treaty, it is interesting to note, provided, among other things, that all Christian women in Persian harems should be freed. However, notwithstanding the new borders, a significant number of small towns and villages, such as Salmas (birthplace of the author Raffi) and territories including early

---

*Emma Aghayan was a member of the Iranian Parliament from 1974 to 1978.

Christian churches such as St. Stephanos and St. Thadeus, all of which were part of historical Armenia, remained in Iran.

The newly drawn borders caused voluntary population shifts. Many Armenians chose to live on the Russian-controlled side of the border in Armenia, Georgia, and Russia, which after all were Christian nations. The decision by many Armenians to live on "the other side" does not imply that Iran did not welcome Armenians in its midst. In fact, Armenians in Iran enjoyed a high quality of life, and they prospered culturally and economically in northwest Iran and in the city of Tabriz, in particular. While these Armenians did not belong to the diaspora, a second group of Armenians lived in the region of Ispahan in Central Iran, having been brought there in the early seventeenth century. These Armenians originating in historical Armenia had been forcefully displaced as a result of the wars between Ottoman Turkey and Iran. They lived and prospered in that region and contributed greatly to its development.

IRANIAN POLITICAL DEVELOPMENTS

Armenian life in its Persian homeland has been greatly impacted by political events affecting Iran. Therefore, a few words on recent Iranian political events as they affected Armenian interests are in order.

The Constitution of 1906 and Parliament

The foundations for democracy in Iran were laid down by the Constitution of 1906. This Constitution provided for a constitutional monarchy, together with a legislative branch consisting of a Parliament (Majlis) with members elected by national suffrage.

In order for the voice of the religious minorities to be heard, they were allocated four seats in Parliament: 2 for the Armenians, 1 for the Jews, and 1 for the Zoroastrians. The representatives of the minorities were full-fledged members of Parliament, emphasizing issues concerning their communities but also participating fully in debates on national issues. Among one of the early parliamentarians was my future father-in-law, Dr. Alexander Aghayan, a prominent Western-educated young lawyer who occupied one of the early seats.

The Pahlavi Dynasty

After two centuries of rule, the Ghajar dynasty was succeeded by the Pahlavi dynasty, starting with Reza Shah in 1926 and ending with his son Mohammed Reza Shah in 1979. During this period Iran progressed on many fronts. Political power that had hitherto been somewhat diffused throughout the nation in the hands of feudal landlords was gradually centralized, and governmental institutions on the Western model were created to service and support a growing and increasingly complex society.

Schools

Many tuition-free schools were opened on the basis of the French model. The uniform teaching programs mandated by the Ministry of Education affected the Armenian schools as well, but they continued to have much leeway to structure their own program. These schools had until then followed their own Armenian curriculum with very little emphasis on the Farsi language. Under the current rules, all schools, including Armenians schools, are strictly subject to the uniform program. The result has been that the Armenian youth has a lessened opportunity to learn about Armenian issues and the Armenian language. On the other hand, the standardization has allowed Armenian students to participate fully in the national education system, with easier access to universities in Iran and abroad.

Women in Iranian Society, Voting Rights

Since the early thirties, Iranian women, who enjoyed far more rights than women in other Islamic countries, were forbidden to wear the veil or *tchador*, and men were prohibited to wear their traditional hats and costumes. In the early sixties, women were given the right to vote and become members of Parliament. These rights continue to date and have not been abrogated by the current Islamic Republic.

WORLD WAR II AND MY INITIAL INTERESTS

The occupation of Iran by allied forces during the Second World War had a lasting impact on me and on Iranians in general. From my early youth I was an active member of "Ararat Miutiun." My four brothers and I attended Iranian schools, not Armenian. I was fluent in Farsi, Armenian, French, and English. I made and kept very close friendships during my school years. I was naturally drawn to politics, and had increasing exposure to it after my marriage to Shahen Aghayan, son of Dr. Alexander Aghayan, who had been recurrently elected to Parliament during critical periods of recent Iranian history. After living in Argentina and Brazil for a few years, we returned to Iran in the early sixties.

THE SIXTIES AND SEVENTIES

Slowly, our generation was starting to occupy important positions in government. One welcome development was the appointment of Amir Abbas Hoveyda as Prime Minister, a post he kept for thirteen years. Mr. Hoveyda was a close friend of my husband's from their school days at Brussels University. This allowed my husband and me to more easily communicate to the Government the particular needs of the Armenian community, and to obtain fast and satisfactory solutions.

In the sixties I had no particular interest in running for Parliament. My late brother-in-law, Felix Aghayan, was then a member of Parliament representing the Armenian community, and I was able to assist Armenian causes as a private citizen. An example of my activities as a private citizen was my managing to obtain significant funding from the Prime Minister's discretionary budget to complete the Ararat Sporting Stadium, a sports and social club catering exclusively to Armenians.

In the early seventies, my brother-in-law, Felix Aghayan, decided to run for the Senate as a representative from Tehran generally, not as a representative of the Armenian minority. There were no special representatives of religious minorities in the Senate, as opposed to the Parliament. Felix Aghayan ran for and won one of the twelve senatorial seats for Tehran.

THE 1975 ELECTIONS

The 1975 parliamentary elections were approaching, and the Armenian community had to decide whom to support. Before going any further, I think it is important to correct any false impression that may exist about the freedom of elections during the late Shah's period. It is true that extremist groups, such as communist activists, were banned from running for Parliament, and also true that, before the land reforms of the sixties, feudal landlords would be effectively guaranteed a seat by vote of their peasants. However, the vast majority of parliamentarians, while well known to their constituencies, were virtually unknown to, and not subject to the control of, the central government.

With the support of old friends, and my early association with the Ararat Miutiun, I declared my candidacy and opened my electoral campaign on the following basis:

1. My candidacy was proposed and supported in press editorials.

2. Gatherings were organized in Armenian schools which catered to over 20,000 students and around which centered

the social lives of their families. This gave me access to virtually all Armenian families.

My commitment to the Armenian cause was already established due to my prior activities as a private citizen. From my own beliefs and experience, and from my interaction with Armenians of all socio-economic levels, I came to a better understanding that what the Armenian minority needed most was to preserve its language, culture, and religion, while not isolating itself from Iranian society. This required concentration on issues dealing with schools, churches, and sports/social organizations. In the meantime the needs of particular individuals and communities would also have to be met on a case per case basis. While many male members of Parliament had other concurrent occupations, I knew that I could devote all my time and energies to this job, and perhaps achieve much more than my male colleagues.

I faced many questions during my campaign, including my town by town visits to every community in the north of Iran where Armenians lived. I did not over promise, tried to keep things on a realistic level, and ended up achieving more than I could have dreamed of. Armenian women generally supported my candidacy and assisted my campaign. I am particularly grateful to them for having supported me in my quest for a position that hitherto only men had occupied.

MY ACTIVITIES AS A PARLIAMENTARIAN

Eventually, I was elected by a great majority. Never had Armenians cast their votes in such large numbers, and I suppose much of that was due to the large turnout of women, who had had no particular desire to vote in the past. I became one of twenty women deputies out of a total of 265 deputies.

In Parliament, I joined the housing and foreign relations committees. The latter gave me the opportunity to meet members of the U.S. House of Representatives and Senate, as well as to develop a rapport with the U.S. diplomatic staff. Furthermore, as a member and secretary general of the French-speaking union in Parliament, I was invited to visit the National Assembly in Paris and celebrate their July 14th celebrations in 1976.

Now a few words about my achievements. My status as a deputy in Parliament permitted me to contact any administrative authority on an official basis, and to systematically attend to the needs of the Armenian community at large as well as specific instances where an individual or a particular community needed relief from a government agency that was mired in red tape.

Churches

One of the most urgent projects that needed attention was the ongoing restoration of the two early Christian churches, St. Thadeus and St. Stepanos. The latter is located south of the Arax River. Already prior to being elected to Parliament, I had been approached by Empress Farah through Prime Minister Hoveyda to find a way to restore these churches, which had been abandoned since World War II. As this type of restoration was not within my or anyone else's expertise in Iran, I suggested that UNESCO's help be enlisted. UNESCO then assigned a French-Armenian architect, the late Edouard Utudjian, to study the restoration project and make recommendations. After careful studies, a French stone worker or *tailleur de pierre* was assigned to the task, and he stayed and worked on site for seven years.

Cultural Exchange

Parallel to the above activities, I arranged for French-Armenian youth to come and meet our Armenian youth and spend some time camping together at St. Thadeus without interfering with the ongoing work. I obtained all the necessary assistance from Prime Minister Hoveyda and the local Governor, including the supply of tents, field kitchens, medical services, and the like. This joint spiritual experience eventually led to the formation of the Terre et Culture (Land and Culture) Association by the French-Armenian youth. Not only was this outing a culturally enriching experience, but it also helped our western brothers and sisters to better appreciate the effort that Iran was making to preserve the cultural heritage and religious structures of the Armenian minority.

Sports and Social Institutions

The Ararat Stadium and Cultural Center, which consists of a grandiose structure, was then in its completion phase.

Armenian Schools

The tens of Armenian schools which were either free or highly subsidized were facing great difficulties in meeting payroll, social security, and pension obligations. These financial problems were substantially alleviated as a result of bringing the matter to the attention of the Ministry of Culture and Education, which increased their funding of these schools.

Electrification and other Municipal Services

Another task which I accomplished was the electrification of remote Armenian villages. After much effort in walking these demands through a maze of central and regional governmental bureaucracies, and much day-to-day follow-up work, electricity was finally brought to these villages. By making the local population more comfortable, this perhaps also helped in discouraging the depopulation of some of these ancient localities in favor of big cities. Also, I personally took the Mayor of Tehran with his retinue of experts through the Armenian districts and persisted until the streets were properly paved, running water and sewer lines installed, and other municipal services fully extended to the areas in question.

It is not feasible to enumerate all the activities which I undertook while in Parliament. However, I hope to have given a general idea of what is involved in representing the interests of the Armenian community in Iran. What sets Armenian interests apart from the general interests of the Iranian population is the need to preserve and promote religious and cultural institutions and customs so as not to be diluted within the Iranian population at large. This is a delicate task, however, as Armenians in Iran are Iranians and have to be perceived as such and not as guests in a foreign country. This balancing act between Armenian lifestyle and general Iranian living is what I consider myself to have been particularly apt at, and which helped me in communicating with my non-Armenian Iranian friends, who were so helpful in getting things done.

ISLAMIC REVOLUTION AND POST-REVOLUTIONARY ACTIVITIES

The Revolution of 1979 ended my mandate six months prior to the end of my four-year elected term. In December 1978, as Iran was in considerable turmoil, I left for New York for a three-week stay with my children. That was the last I saw of Iran for the next fifteen years, until I briefly visited the country two years ago. All our possessions were confiscated by the new government.

In the post-Revolutionary period, I travelled to Pakistan with my personal resources to save young Armenian boys whose parents had sent them across the border to escape military service in the Iran-Iraq war, a pattern that was followed by all Iranian families who had the wherewithal to do so. These boys, together with some girls between ages of 15-25, were simply stranded and forgotten in Pakistan with no money, no medical services, and no housing. Having simply escaped from Iran, they did not have any papers, and no country was in a great hurry to take them in. After spending many days going over and documenting as many individual cases as I could, and with the able assistance of the United Nations and other influential persons, I was able to get many of these stranded Armenians into France, Canada, and the United States, as political refugees or under various other classifications. Senator Robert Dole in the United States was particularly concerned and helpful with respect to the plight of the Armenians, and I will forever be in his debt for his efforts.

CONCLUSION

I hope to have succeeded in relaying at least some flavor of my activities in the context of pre-Revolutionary Iran. As governments come and go, it is important for Armenians in all nations where they are minorities to keep involved and build bridges to the successive power structures within their respective countries. In addition to successful business activities, Armenians would greatly benefit from participating in their countries' politics, and I hope to have set a least a modest example of that.

Participating in the Political Process in the United States

Lily Ring Balian*

The topic for discussion, "Gaining Power and Influence in Government and Business," could read as the title of my life, because I have been spending my career doing this. And the way to be successful is to realize that it starts with you, no one but you, and you are the only person who can develop and promote your image.

And again, consider the theme "Armenian Women in a Changing World." It is important that all of us, men and women, develop new roles in a changing environment. Women need to take off their aprons and get involved. They don't really need to take off their aprons, just ask someone at home to hold their aprons—to free them to bring their unique talents, their energy, their creativity, and their rich cultural heritage to the policy-making organizations and institutions in their country, wherever it may be, and in their communities. To get involved in the political process and to influence political leaders starts at the local level, no matter where you reside.

One of my messages today is that we all have a stake in our communities. There is a need for all of us to become involved so that we can have real input into the issues and

*Lily Ring Balian is a political consultant and chairs the California Commission on the Status of Women.

policies which inevitably determine the destinies of future generations. It is important for each of us to make a difference in the development of a better community for our families and our children.

We can no longer pay attention to the enunciation of certain statements that have kept Armenians in a certain kind of position—a position that can be embarrassing when one is a new arrival in a country of one's choice. The time is long overdue, and we should no longer be complacent or passive about the way in which we are viewed. We need to take positive action to dispel the perception and the image prevalent in some areas that Armenians are non-productive members of society, that Armenians take advantage of certain social services and welfare programs, that they keep to their own culture and heritage and are not active participants in their communities.

But you can change that, it starts with you. You can develop strategies to improve your status, the role of Armenian women in your community, while still retaining the richness of our cultural heritage.

First, you need to get involved in community activities, public agencies, and organizations. And to get involved means to be an active participant. The term "grass roots" means at your local level, in your own neighborhoods. Women have a great opportunity in America through the local schools and parent teachers associations. In the United States it is important that women participate in voter registration drives, no matter what your political affiliation. The first thing to do is to register to vote. Wherever you decide to live, that country needs and will continue to need your God-given talents and abilities. There is no better way to demonstrate your commitment as a citizen. In some parts of America, you can offer your house as a polling place. What better way to meet your neighbors, demonstrate that you are concerned active citizens, that you share a common goal, that you believe in the system of your country, and that you believe in the political process?

You know the organizations in your country, in your community. An exciting way to get involved is to participate in election campaigns. You volunteer your energy and hard work to your church and many other Armenian organizations, and you can direct that same energy, vitality, and talent to community and volunteer participation.

But you need to bring more than *kufta* or *paklava* to these meetings. You need to be actively involved. Volunteer to serve on boards. Offer to chair a committee or undertake a particular project. The most effective way to participate in the process is to help in a campaign. You can make telephone calls, walk neighborhoods and precincts, and the more you do, the more you become visible. And since we were all endowed at an early age with a strong sense of ethnic pride, you become visible as an Armenian.

Secondly, it is important to understand that, once you are an active participant in any organization or group, your effectiveness depends on your ability to gain the respect of the people you are working with, some of whom may be adversaries. (I don't want to use the word "enemies.")

If you are discussing a particular issue or a particular decision to be made, your real challenge lies in enlisting the support of others, some of whom may be opposed or disagree with your view. You may be dealing with some people who are prejudiced or biased. You have to understand the importance of coalitions and alliances. You need to build a network of support, and on occasion you may even join your opponents, your enemies, your adversaries. Your presence, your purpose, is to get things done, and sometimes you may win and be successful, and sometimes you may not, but at least you were part of the decision-making process.

I can tell you I would have fallen flat on my face in the business world if I had spent my energies becoming overly sensitive to snide remarks or if I had responded angrily when someone disagreed with me. You have to have the strength and courage to stand up for what you believe in, and yet at the same time you can't be hostile or nasty or whine or whimper or, heaven forbid, lose your temper. Always deal with your adversaries or opponents with grace and dignity, or laughter, or with food (offer them some *choereg*). And tell them, "I don't expect everybody in the world to agree with what I am doing or what I am saying, and it is quite evident from your behavior towards me that you don't agree with me." But then, no two of us are alike, so then you just look at them very nicely, smile, and say, "Maybe next time," and go about your business. In this way people will understand that your contribution was not for your personal benefit, but for the benefit of the job that has to be done—whatever it is. It is a slow, grinding process. But you are building your credibility. You are developing a network and, last but not least, you are demonstrating by your behavior, by your actions, and by your attitude, that you are part of the community or the city or state or country, and that you are willing to work together to get things done. No one else can do this for you.

I was fortunate in my career, I had a mentor. I worked for a man in California who was the district attorney for many years and then elected to be attorney-general of the State of California—the Chief Lawyer. Then he ran for governor, and unfortunately he lost, but I had sixteen productive and rewarding years with him. And that is where I learned to be a professional, something I worked at every day. He was a tremendous leader and administrator. He would never react in an angry fashion, or be critical, or be rude. He would act positively, he would respect other people's comments and listen. If someone disagreed with him on occasion, he would respect their judgment, and at some point later on they might agree with him. A successful politician develops skills of conciliation. He did not hold a grudge or harbor any ill will, or punish someone for disagreeing with him. He would select people to fill important positions in his office based on their qualifications and ability to get the job done, whether they were his friends or not and whether they supported him for election or not.

He was my entré into the political world. He opened doors for me to gain visibility and exposure. He and his wife encouraged me to become actively involved in campaigns. They convinced me that I had more potential than I realized. They motivated me to do more, seek more, and become more. Through him I volunteered to help in former President Ronald Reagan's campaign, and after volunteering for only three days, I was asked to go to Washington and work on the presidential campaign in 1980. That opened doors in Washington, and I had a wonderful experience. I was rewarded by the President and received a commission on the National Advisory Council for Adult Education, a position I held for six years. When I returned to California, I was recruited by Northrop Grumman Corporation, to work as their government relations director.

And here is my third point, and this is important for women: I encourage all of you to get involved in campaigns. As you may know, I received an appointment from California Governor Pete Wilson as one of the fifteen members of the Commission on the Status of Women. That appointment came about as a result of my volunteering to work on his first campaign for governor. I offered to chair a committee to organize Women for Wilson, to spread the word that he was concerned about women's issues, that he was pro-choice. I spent evenings making telephone calls on his behalf. I became a surrogate speaker. I sent letters to women inviting them to participate in his campaign, many of them Armenian women. When he was elected, he had made a campaign promise to involve and appoint more women and minorities to positions in his administration. I was offered this commission. I mention this to motivate you, to encourage you to get involved in campaigns.

I also encourage you to support other women candidates by contributing to their campaigns. Your husband, if you have one, shouldn't be the only one to write checks for hundreds or thousands of dollars. Women should do the same. You can volunteer and work, but we need to learn to dig deep into our pockets and also give money to help women get elected.

Of course, I mean Armenian women. There aren't many Armenian women in politics. In our legislature in California, with 180 members of the Assembly and Senate, there is one Armenian woman.

There is another way to bring visibility to Armenians. Armenians who volunteered and assisted Governor George Deukmejian of California received many appointments, and I enjoy seeing many names ending with "ian" still in government, serving in judicial positions, and taking an active part in the political process.

In fact, when the President of Armenia, Levon Ter Petrossian, visited California recently, I was very fortunate to be invited by Governor Wilson, with four other Armenians, to demonstrate to our President that we were contributing citizens in the State of California, and to call his attention to the fact that Wilson had appointed Armenian women to important posts.

I know that there are many people in the audience today who are actively engaged in political campaigns. I am again involved in Governor Wilson's re-election campaign. I am here to urge you to get involved in any campaign, in any capacity.

Let me tell you about the Commission on the Status of Women. The commission was established by the California Legislature, which found that, despite that fact that women apparently have greater equality in California than in many states, they still are not able to contribute to society according to their full potential. The commission was created with a view to developing recommendations which will enable women to make the maximum contribution to society.

Of course that refers to Armenian women as well. We are living in a changing world, and the rapidly changing conditions in the world today pose new challenges and offer new opportunities to Armenian women. There have been significant changes in Armenian family life, and more Armenian women are entering the work force than ever before. Armenian women are entering political office; they are gaining power and influence in government and in business. They are increasing their visibility and promoting their equal role in the community. They are involved in women's health issues, particularly women's reproductive health, and they are making a difference in the development of a better world for themselves and their families and their children.

Recently, an Armenian woman in Boston, Massachusetts, Janet Jeghelian, ran for the United States Senate seat held by Senator Edward M. (Ted) Kennedy. I mean to say she dared to run against Senator Kennedy. She was bold.

I applaud her. She got visibility. She had the opportunity to appear on the media, talk shows, give speeches, and she brought her name and her qualifications before the public. I hope she will run again for public office, and maybe the next time she will have a better chance. But she dared.

And she is opening the door for other women. She is demonstrating by her action that the time has come when women must not be shy or reluctant. Many women have come to realize that they too, not just men, are compassionate human beings, well suited to formulate policy and make decisions, become proactive in the community and, last but not least, that women can be successful candidates for public office and can lead. Former British Prime Minister Margaret

Thatcher declared that in politics, if you want anything said, ask a man, but if you want anything done, ask a woman.

In conclusion, to summarize: changes do not come about in some kind of vacuum. Get involved in the community at any level, in any civic or local group, but be an active participant. You need to be a participant, not a pawn that someone else can manipulate and make decisions for you. Once you are an active participant, you have to develop a network of support, build coalitions and allies, and make friends. It's important to understand that you can't do anything alone and to be a true professional in your behavior and in your attitude.

Don't be impatient, because in the long term, if you continue to stay involved and continue to be visible, you will be benefiting your community, your family, your children, and most of all, you will be benefiting all Armenians. And we can continue to be justifiably proud of our Armenian heritage.

But, ultimately, what is more important, we will craft and develop a life, a work, whose meaning and legacy are larger than ourselves. We will speak up, resonate deeply, and make a strong impact, with this, our extraordinary generation of women.

There is power in a woman's voice. We are fortunate that we are living at a turning point in women's political history. There has been a social revolution that women have created over the past twenty-five years. Women need to be visible in that revolution and in that way become educators for the next generation.

Women can no longer be ambivalent about political life. We have seen that it is still an "old boys" network throughout the world.

The optimistic illusion that one can change the world is difficult to resist. There is a great deal of evidence that individuals can make a difference inside the mainstream of politics, and when I say politics, I mean building bridges to government and getting involved in organizations, associations, and administrations, where you can make a difference.

A woman, with her gender and her conscious feminism, can affect everything. You won't see a man focus on women's issues. Men don't author legislation on breast cancer or women's health issues. It has to be woman who initiate these programs. And when a woman is in a position of power, during her tenure she can appoint more women.

When a woman is in power, she is no longer at the periphery or at the edge, but in the center. Women who enter the political world or policy making organizations bring new perspectives and can make a difference.

The British Experience

Odette Bazil*

THE BRITISH PARLIAMENT

The British Parliament, known as "The Mother of all Parliaments" and now meeting in the Palace of Westminster commonly known as the Houses of Parliament, originated in the King's Councils summoned by English Kings in the eleventh and twelfth centuries. These Councils were attended by various officials together with the King's Ministers. They usually met in churches and cathedrals, and this is the reason why the sitting arrangement in Parliament Chambers resembles the one in churches, contrary to other parliaments where seats are placed in semi-circles. By 1236 these councils were called parliaments and at that time Simon de Montfort, one of the nobles, suggested that "the representatives of the knights should be summoned to assist the nobles and the king" in Parliament. This is regarded as the origin of Western democracy in that for the first time people sat in Parliament as the representatives of others and not in their own individual right. By the end of the fourteenth century these representatives met separately and became the House of Commons, with their own Speaker and their own Clerk.

During the same period the Lords also acquired an identity as a separate House or Dommus Superiore or Upper

*Odette Bazil is Honorary Secretary of the British-Armenian All-Party Parliamentary Group.

House. It is only around the sixteenth century that the term House of Lords became normally used. Membership of the Lords became hereditary and confined only to men. In 1876 a new law called the Appellate Jurisdiction enabled sovereigns to create Life Peerages, which are titles bestowed in recognition of services to the Crown or exceptional achievement, but these titles are not hereditary and last only while the recipient is alive or in office. To date almost 600 such Peerages have been created. Caroline Cox received one in 1983 when she became Baroness Cox of Queensbury, and Margaret Thatcher received hers in 1992 and became known as Baroness Thatcher of Kesteven in the County of Lincolnshire. I am happy that I had the good fortune to attend her investiture and must report that there was not one empty seat at the Lords that day.

In 1834 the old Palace of Westminster was largely destroyed by fire and was rebuilt between 1840 and 1860; also the Chamber was burned out by enemy actions in 1941 and the only remaining vestige of the old Chamber is an Arch, flanked by the statue of Churchill and called the Churchill Arch.

I can assure you that nowhere but within the Houses of Parliament can one feel the overpowering presence of the past and nowhere else do the hundreds of pictures of past Kings and Queens come to life than along these majestic corridors and inside these sumptuous rooms, where the destiny of Britain, the Commonwealth, and also maybe the world is shaped and decided.

THE WORKINGS OF THE BRITISH PARLIAMENT

I do not believe that anyone would attempt to describe the workings of such intricate, complex, and huge organization in only twenty minutes or even twenty hours, but within my modest limitations I will try to share with you the insight that I have acquired during the past three years. The United

Kingdom Parliament consists of the Queen, the House of Lords, and the House of Commons. All three work together to carry out the work of Parliament which is: making laws, examining the work of the Government, controlling finances, examining European proposals, debating current affairs, and hearing appeals.

The House of Commons is formed by 651 Members who are elected at a General Election which takes place every five years. They represent 651 constituencies to which they refer as their "Seats." A General Election can also be called by the Government to decide on a vital issue. A by-election happens only in one constituency when its representing Member of Parliament (MP) either dies, retires, or resigns. We witnessed many such cases in the last few years, where resignations were mainly due to sex-related indiscretions.

The party that wins the most seats forms the Government. At present there are 333 Conservative, 269 Labour, and 20 Liberal Democrat MPs, with only 59 women MPs. The Government is formed by one hundred MPs of the winning Party and twenty of its most senior Members, who form the Cabinet. There are currently two women in Prime Minister John Major's Cabinet, both representing offices that are normally allocated to women: health, and education and welfare. Compared to the one woman Minister in the Armenian Cabinet, I believe that Armenia is not doing very badly indeed.

The Labour Party is known as the "Opposition Party." Its job is to challenge the Government, make it explain its policies, and check that it does its work properly. The opposition is extremely important in the working of the British Parliamentary System; this is clearly shown by the fact that the Opposition is recognized as "Her Majesty's Opposition."

Parliament can limit the power of Government by voting

against its proposed laws, by restricting the funds which the Government can spend, by challenging the Government in Debates, and by examining the Government's work in committees.

Therefore the power of Government depends on the consent of the governed.

A word-for-word account of what is said in both Houses of Parliament is recorded by a highly skilled team of short-hand writers and stenographers and can be found in the Official Report usually known as Hansards, named after the family who formerly published these reports since 1803, when newspapers were first allocated seats in the Public Gallery. I am happy to report that I am currently researching what has been recorded in these Hansards about Armenia since 1913, just before the Genocide, until today and hopefully will be able to present it in a compiled documentary.

The House of Lords, whose members are know as Peers, are not elected and take their seats by hereditary succession. Their expertise in their own fields gives them the knowledge to act as the final court of appeal on points of law for the whole of the United Kingdom in Civil Cases, and for England, Wales, and Northern Ireland in Criminal Cases. The judicial work of the House is largely separated from its other functions.

The work of the House of Lords is divided into: Supreme Court of Appeal, debates on matters of public interest, revision of Public Bills (these are drafts destined to become law), initiation of public legislation, scrutiny of the executive, private legislation, European Community committees, science and technology committees, and other select committees.

The Speaker of the House of Lords is the Lord Chancellor. He is the highest paid official in both Houses, with a salary of £106,750, while the Prime Minister receives nothing for this office. But having appointed himself as First Lord of the Treasury, his salary is £76,234 and the Opposition Leader's is £59,736.

The Lord Chancellor is a Member of the Government with a seat in the Cabinet. Therefore he does not remain politically neutral, while the Speaker of the House of Commons has to give up his or her affiliation to any political party in order to remain politically neutral. The major ceremony of the Parliamentary Year is the State Opening of Parliament by the Queen, which is performed every year in the House of Lords. This is not only a sumptuous display of British pageantry at its best, it is also the occasion for Parliament to reopen after the summer recess and for the Queen to deliver her speech, read from her throne, where she unveils the policy of the government for the year ahead. It is a policy that has been written jointly with the Prime Minister and is the result of lengthy discussions in his Cabinet. Until this speech is made and subsequently debated, neither House can conduct any business.

THE MECHANISM OF LOBBYING

Let me briefly describe to you how our British-Armenian All-Party Parliamentary Group came into existence and carried on its business during the past years. Since 1989 Lord Shannon, along with many other illustrious personalities, has been a Patron of the Anglo-Armenian Association, a cultural organization. Almost every day I was sending him newspaper clippings relating to Armenia, its culture, the situation in the earthquake-stricken areas, the war in Karabagh, the massacres in Sumgait, the genocide, and even a book on Armenian cooking, but especially articles and reports about the blockade imposed by Turkey. Baroness Cox also had started presenting reports and delivering lectures. But we could clearly see the urgent need for a larger group to take action and endorse her claims.

To my complete surprise, one day Lord Shannon told me

that, if we wanted positive results, we should start a Parliamentary Group. We founded this on February 14, 1992, then three months later invited Armen Sarkissian, Ambassador from Armenia to the United Kingdom, to be our Patron, and six months later Baroness Cox to become our Vice-Chairman. Lord Molloy of Ealing had already joined as Deputy-Chairman and displayed his solidarity for the Armenians, especially the ones in Ealing. For myself, not being a Parliamentarian, I was allowed to act only in my capacity as Honorary Secretary. Now that we had the required three Parliamentarians to lodge an application, we registered formally and started our work alongside the numerous groups already in existence. Incidently, the Azeris started their Parliamentary Group only in mid-1994.

We printed our letterhead with the Portcullis on the left corner representing the British Parliament and the emblem of the Armenian government on the right corner. For the use of the latter we had to acquire, through Ambassador Sarkissian, the Armenian government's approval. Now a mammoth task was facing us: the task of gaining support from MPs and Peers.

To embark on such a venture and have strong faith in its outcome, I needed the immense love for Armenia that warms my heart, the friendly and expert advice of a friend in power, the genuine and constant concern for the people in Armenia, and the worrying knowledge that my own identity was at risk if Armenia would be no more and if I couldn't call myself an Armenian any longer. I needed that strong belief because there were rebuffs, bitter despairs, and an irritating impatience that sometimes was impossible to repress. Media centers were contacted to provide day-to-day information, newspapers started piling up on my desk (they still do), weekly briefings by Ambassador Sarkissian were giving us the latest news, and his wise counsel was setting the pace for our campaign.

We had gained access to the Parliament's Library, and the Hansards were read everyday. Every Thursday we were and are receiving all that has been reported in the papers about Armenia, Karabagh, Turkey, Azerbaijan, and Iran. With the help of all this information we also found out the names of the Parliamentarians who had, in the past, spoken fairly about Armenia. We studied all 1,851 Members in both Houses. We scrutinized their interests and achievements. Then, after meeting, consulting, and discussing with the members of our council, we chose whom to approach and lobby. I applied for membership to dozens of organizations concerned with public affairs and human rights, attended (and still do) every lecture, debate, conference, and discussion table addressing these issues, because the major part of any lobbying is to be able to inform constantly the person in power and to be able to provide him or her with the best tools available to defend that cause with up-to-date information.

It is through our campaign that we discovered how little even people in political spheres knew about Armenia, yet they knew so much about Turkey. We had to produce maps and books and organize meetings and briefings during which the maps were studied and the situation clearly explained. Even to the friendly MPs approached, the real issue was the war in Karabagh and the displaced Azeri refugees, whereas to us that issue was and still is the blockade of Armenia.

So we had to meet the MPs personally and introduce them to Ambassador Sarkissian, who would brief them using all his diplomatic skills. We had to invite Armenian government officials to come and talk to them. Ultimately *we had to convince them.*

By now, the late half of 1992, we had gained the friendship and support of eight Parliamentarians. This is when we decided to take a Parliamentary delegation to Armenia, at the invitation of the Armenian government, following Ambassador Sarkissian's mediation, in order to show them first-hand the destruction caused by the earthquake, the formidable Azeri war machine, and, more deadly, the tragic death and distress caused by the blockade.

We took them to Karabagh, to the military hospital. I recall one member of the delegation who fainted at the sight of the poignant scene that developed before our eyes in that operating room.

The delegation met the President, the President of the Armenian Parliament, the leaders of Karabagh, government officials, and the people of Yerevan and Giumri. They returned with a totally different insight and, rejecting the Azeri propaganda, they now were ready to lobby the government on our behalf. They called a press conference during which they presented a jointly drawn statement condemning the blockade and in turn informing their colleagues. They began to put questions to the Government, asking for debates during which other MPs briefed by them would stand up and defend our cause.

I remember clearly the debate of October 28, 1993, instigated by Lord Shannon, himself a former Deputy Speaker of the House of Lords for ten years, when Mr. Major walked into the Lords Chamber, where he hadn't been for four years, stood there for eleven minutes—as MPs are not allowed to sit at the Lords, they can only stand outside what is called "the Bar," and listened with total amazement to the most anti-government virulent speech that Lord Shannon had ever delivered, followed by Baroness Cox, who accused the government of double standards. Six Peers joined in the debate and expressed their support. It is during that debate that Baroness Chalker, on behalf of the British government, declared that they were willing to participate at the Minsk Peace process if invited.

We in the group have our doubts about the benefit of such involvement, for the profits from an oil deal with Azerbaijan can be so lucrative that any government would look twice before engaging in blaming Azerbaijan for its actions. We had to learn with bitter disappointment and frustrating anger that agreements with officials can be canceled without reason, that promises can be broken, that the Azeri refugee issue can be thrown at one's face in response to requests for making Turkey lift the blockade, and (if looked closely) one can easily find the connection with British Petroleum and the hope of an Azeri oil deal behind every refusal and every cancellation.

When our Group invited three Armenian MPs to visit London, a meeting at the Foreign Office was organized and, to greet us, along with the high-ranking British official, was a Turkish high-ranking official of the Foreign Office. That Turkish official was the person who was supposed to intervene on our behalf and ask the Turkish Government to lift the blockade! Seldom in my life have I felt such anger and humiliation.

I had never truly realized how valuable the support and campaigning of a Parliamentarian can be until the David Treddenick Affair, in which a disguised reporter posing as a businessman had offered £1,000 to the MP for a question to be put to the government on behalf of his company. Two days later a reporter from the *Daily Mail* called to ask how much we Armenians were paying to have our cause debated so many times in both Houses. Of course we have not, are not, and have never been in the position to remunerate an MP for tabling a question on our behalf. We are merely calling to their conscience by showing them the unacceptable wrong that has been done and by providing them with the information to fight the abuse.

To date, the blockade of Armenia, the sale of arms to Azerbaijan, the decision of the Turkish government to send troops for peace-keeping in Karabagh, and many more issues concerning Armenia have been debated in the British Parliament. On nine occasions our Parliamentarian friends have written to the Foreign Office and protested on our behalf. I must confess that not all our lobbying has been successful, for instance in the case of British sale of arms to Azerbaijan and the despatch of British mercenaries to Karabagh. Although the issues had been debated and Chris Mullins, a Labour MP, had demanded an explanation in one of the national papers, the outcome remained dormant and unaddressed. We met Dennis Canavan MP (Labour), Member of the Scotts Inquiry in charge of investigating the Pergau Dam Affair, and although he was interested in taking up our case and furthering the proceedings, we failed to provide him with the necessary documents as no one had tangible proof. Yet we knew that arms had been delivered and that British mercenaries were helping the Azeris.

To date we have forty-six Parliamentarians who receive our correspondence, whom we meet from time to time, to whom we can present our grievances, and whom we can call our friends. We also have twenty-nine non-Parliamentarian associate members who also receive our correspondence, attend our functions and meetings, and support us with their financial contributions.

A counterpart group, namely the Armenian-British All-Party Parliamentary Group, is in existence within the Armenian Parliament. Their members visit us when possible, and I am very pleased indeed to report that very good relations are creating the occasions for members of both Parliaments—British and Armenian—to visit and converse. Next week, at the invitation of the Armenian Government, a second Parliamentary Delegation will visit Yerevan with delegates representing all three major Political Parties, and we feel very honored that the Deputy-Leader of the Liberal Democrat Party, the Baroness Seear, will be of the visiting party.

As there are currently eight Armenian Embassies either fully operational or in the process of being opened in Europe, and following our Chairman's suggestion and Ambassador Sarkissian's consent, Parliamentary Groups similar to ours will be established in each of these countries, together with the host countries, with eventually the possibility to create a *Pan-Armenian Parliamentary Union* which will hold seminars, exchange information on their respective working procedures, and further the lobbying for the good of Armenia.

In conclusion, may I stress the fact that lobbying should not be restricted and directed only to parliamentarians. Lobbying can be done every day of our lives, in schools, in the workplace, during social encounters, even in churches.

The first step is to assume our own identity, as women and as Armenians, and then to assess in total awareness the contribution we can make to this changing world, by caring for our homeland regardless of party politics, by promoting our culture, our food, our music and our traditions, and by justifying the war in Karabagh and researching the circumstances that have lead our country to war.

If, in order to be fed, an infant has to scream, then let us scream. Let us protest when wrong has been done. Let us every day without relent call upon the Turkish government and ask Prime Minister Ciller to lift that inhumane blockade which is crippling Armenia and killing its children.

For it is ultimately the privilege and duty of every human being to protect its rights.

Women and Politics in Armenia

Hranush Hagopian*

From all corners of the world we are gathered together for this unprecedented meeting where all of us, whatever our differences, have our roots in Armenian soil, our homeland. At this auspicious time we are celebrating the third anniversary of Armenian Independence, the realization of a 600-year dream. Despite all our difficulties and successes, we are full of pride and veneration to have a sovereign Armenia, similar to the United States of America and England. It is remarkable that twenty women from the Armenian Republic can freely participate in these meetings here in London, without any problems and without the difficulties associated previously with the Iron Curtain. Today women from Armenia and the diaspora can come together and work together, something which in the past we could not even think about.

During the difficult conditions that accompanied the transition to an independent Republic, in an enthusiastic election campaign, 248 deputies were elected to the nation's Parliament, of whom only nine were women. It is painfully unfortunate that only three percent of the members of Parliament are women, and if we look at local and regional governments, the situation is even more striking. Only one of the 68 local councils is headed by a woman, Jemma Ananian,

---

*Hranush Hagopian is a deputy in the Parliament of the Armenian Republic and chairs the Committee on Family and Social Welfare.

mayor of Ijevan and a member of Parliament, who is here with us in London.

In contrast, if we look at the situation in the First Republic of 1918-1920, eight percent of the members of parliament were women. And to its credit, under the difficult conditions of the time, the Republic of 1918-1920 was one of the first nations to give women the right to vote and to be elected to the highest organs of government. Moreover, women achieved legal and constitutional rights equal to those of the men. Now, only after seventy-five years, do women once again have the opportunity to participate in the political life of an independent republic. This is a great victory, not only for Armenian women, but for the Armenian Republic.

And today, when there is so much talk about discrimination against women, when the United Nations is preparing specific documents detailing the rights of women, when international conferences and congresses are being organized, at all levels of government in the Armenian Republic, from the President down to the lowest level, attention is given to the condition of women, the rights of pregnant women, and the needs of children and the handicapped. Women's rights are no different from the rights of men. They must have the same value and should be defended equally by the government.

The Armenian woman, who carries a burden equal to that of a man, who holds a gun the same way as a man does and fights against the enemy, deserves special care as a symbol of family and homeland. For this reason the Republic Parliament, upon my initiative, established April 7 as a holiday to commemorate motherhood and beauty.

And just as women participate in government activities, in the same way they should have political influence. The United Nations documents state that woman is equal to man, can participate equally in political and social activity, and can hold any responsible position. In Armenia, in these difficult days, the government is not always using the full potential of women and taking advantage of women's qualities of diligence, attention, gentleness, talent, instinct, and intelligence. Potential women leaders face a difficult road. There are few women in the high levels of government. There are only three women assistants to the President, the Prime Minister has only five, and there is not a single woman in the other branches of government. There are no women in high-level positions in the banks, in the Constitutional Court, and only one in the diplomatic service. In government offices there are 119 women out of 282 employoos, but only four head an office. We can continue to cite similar statistics to indicate that women have only a very slight influence on the decisions made by the government. The government is not using the full talents of women in the development of society, in the stability of the state, and for peace. On the other hand, women bear an especially heavy burden in health care (80 percent), in education (75 percent), and in culture.

It is important to note, however, that even if women had equal rights with men, our situation would continue to be difficult. The woman is first a wife and mother and carries a heavy responsibility in the home. If we look at the results of a poll conducted in 1994, we find that 91 percent of women want to have a family, 86 percent want to work, but only 10 percent want to be leaders. Among the women polled, 52 percent are not members of any party or political organization and only 18 percent are politically active (compared to 35.5 percent for the men). Another interesting statistic: asked about the more desirable characteristics for Armenian women, the responses were as follows: 64 percent cited resilience, 46 percent, organizing ability, 40 percent, diligence, 32 percent, national sentiments. Thus equality does not have the same meaning for women that it has for men. The solution of this question will have a major impact on the development of humanity.

The General Assembly of the United Nations has declared full equality for women and men, to make certain that women participate in all branches of government and in social and cultural affairs. The importance of the role of women in diplomatic ranks should be accepted, as well as their potential in social organizations.

In Armenia we are building a democratic state. This is our fate as a nation, and our generation is fortunate to have the responsibility for this important process. One evidence of democracy is that today we are establishing unions, organizations, foundations, and associations of all kinds. We have 400 organizations of which twenty are for women. With these activities, the Armenian woman is attempting to participate in the social and political life of our homeland. We have today women leaders who are able to organize and to lead large women's associations which have an impact on all Armenian women. The greatest responsibility is to defend women's rights and to cooperate with our sisters in the diaspora and to be able to speak out in conferences, such as this and especially the 1995 United Nations Conference in Beijing.

A large part of women's activity lies in the field of welfare, helping other human beings. Women are active in organizing orphanages, in programs for former soldiers, invalids, and families who have lost soldiers. In these areas can be seen women's love and care. In this way women make life more gentle and comfortable. Many Armenian women of the diaspora, through benevolent and religious organizations, are helping our poorer population. One example is Jenia Aidinian Rezaieh of Los Angeles, Executive Director of the Foundation for Children's Homes in Armenia, of which I am a member. This small, gentle women is a ball of fire, having been responsible for the establishment of six orphanages and also a program for homeless families. As a result over 7,000 families, artists, and children have benefited. Similarly many women who are with us today, such as Rita Balian, Flora Dunanians, Elizabeth Aghbabian, Savey Tufenkian, Hermine Janoyan, Nora Nercessian, and many others, are engaged in programs to improve life in the homeland.

The voice of women should be heard in the highest levels of our government. We should have a clear and strong influence on policy. Without the participation of women, there cannot be democracy. Let me tell you under what conditions women work. We are creating a new, free republic, with democracy, with reform, but all of these are accompanied by many difficulties. We have many problems: the blockade by Azerbaijan and Turkey, the war situation in Nagorno-Karabagh. For over six years the people of Armenia, particularly the women and children, have suffered from the effects of the fighting. Women do not have heat, light, enough food, but somehow they manage to take care of the families, their homeland. And when the Armenian woman has a child under these most difficult conditions, it is because she realizes the importance of children for the survival of the nation. According to an old saying, there are three important values in the world: our daily bread, which gives us strength and health; wisdom, which provides nourishment for the mind and soul; and woman, who does not allow the thread of life to be cut.

Despite some improvement in the Armenian economy, the quality of life continues to be very poor. In July 1994 the average salary of the population was $7 per month. Inflation is very high, and many live under almost unbearable conditions. Many people are unemployed—seven percent according to official statistics. Of the unemployed workers, 64 percent are women. Women are losing their economic position and are finding it impossible to begin their own businesses. And when they are not economically independent, they cannot be active participants in government. It is essential to begin planning economic projects that will benefit women. If women are able to participate equally in building our society, if they put their considerable talents to work, they will be able to overcome obstacles, to find power within themselves to overcome obstacles.

We therefore present the following program of action:

1. International resolutions regarding women should be recognized and enforced in Armenia, and our women should be educated to learn their rights.

2. Women should be given the opportunity to participate in all levels of life: social, political, economic, and scientific.

3. Insure the participation of women in all levels of government. The goal should be 50 percent participation of women in all branches of government: city, town, and local.

4. Establish specific departments that will provide an opportunity to fight discrimination.

5. Improve the economic position of women, make certain that they participate in the market economy, and do everything to insure their economic independence.

6. Improve women's health care and make available modern methods of medical treatment.

7. Make use of the potential of women's talent and capabilities to establish peace and to end the blockade of Armenia and Karabagh.

In the last analysis, the establishment of a true and lasting peace will create the conditions for us to build a new society. There is not a woman who does not want peace. We have started a movement for peace; we want the current cease-fire to develop into a true and lasting peace with secure borders for our nation. Only in this way can Armenia reach its potential as a nation and can we reach our potential as women.

The Role of International Organizations

Nariné Sahakian*

As a governmental official, I am involved in a wide variety of assignments dealing with the management and coordination of assistance and development programs. Aid coordination and management are primarily concerned with obtaining, allocating, and managing aid resources made available to support public sector programs over which the government has direct management responsibility.

Let me present a brief description of the current economic situation in Armenia.

The transition to a modern market-driven economy is hampered by the legacy of the past. The central planning system had devastating consequences for the economy, and not for the economy alone. In particular the disintegration of established economic relations and the lack of tradition and experience in independent administration imposed an extremely difficult situation. In addition to these common difficulties faced by all transition economies, Armenia has unique problems. First, in the aftermath of the December 1988 earthquake, over 25,000 people lost their lives and whole towns and villages were leveled to the ground. Our country is still experiencing the effects of the disaster. The industrial plants and fuel pipelines in the earthquake zone

---

*Nariné Sahakian is chief expert of the Foreign Investment and Aid Coordination Department, Ministry of the Economy, Republic of Armenia.

need restoration. Despite assistance received from many countries and non-governmental organizations (NGO's), a tremendous amount of reconstruction remains to be done. This has placed a heavy burden on the economy and has put considerable strain on the budget.

Armenia has suffered the sharpest fall in output of any former Soviet republic. Gross Domestic Product (GDP) declined by 15 percent in 1993, following a 52 percent fall in 1992. In the first half of 1994 real GDP increased by 2-3 percent compared to the same period in 1993. Nevertheless living standards have fallen. Average real wages have plummeted. In June 1994 the average wage in the state sector was about $2 a month and $4-5 economy-wide. An estimated 12 percent of the labor force were on short-time working schedules or on forced leave. Much of the population is living on remittances from the diaspora, humanitarian aid, and income from informal activity.

The government of Armenia is requesting substantial assistance from the international community to support the transition to a market economy, to help reverse the dra-matic decline in economic activity since the collapse of the Soviet Union, and to mitigate the hardships caused by the fall in family income levels and by the present economic blockade. Over the next few years aid will be required for humanitarian assistance, balance of payments and import support, technical assistance, and for financing the public sector investment program. Already considerable assistance is being received from a number of donor agencies of which the World Bank, European Union (EU), and USAID represent the largest programs. In addition the government is receiving significant financial support for its programs from the Armenian diaspora, especially in programs identifying humanitarian needs for Armenia. These are food, fuel, and medicines. In addition education, water and sanitation systems, and the shelter and protection of refugees and Internally Displaced

People (IDP) are needs to be addressed.

The weaker and most vulnerable sections of the population are critically dependent on humanitarian assistance for food, as they are unable to afford to buy necessary quantities at even the present subsidized prices. The Humani-tarian Assistance Commission of the government of Armenia has identified approximately 1.5 million people in need of assistance. This includes an estimated 871,600 children under the age of 16, as well as 150,00 refugees and IDP's, and 400,000 other vulnerable people. The government has also identified school feeding programs as a priority area needing aid.

The shortage of energy and the severity of the winter make humanitarian assistance in the supply of fuel, especially kerosene, which is used both for heating and cooking, essential to Armenia. To try to address the root cause of the problem, the government has plans in 1995 to reopen the nuclear power plant at Medzamor to alleviate the energy situation. It also has a program to rehabilitate the hydro-power station in the country, which needs assistance.

The health situation requires that the supply of medicines be a prime component of the humanitarian assistance program for Armenia. In addition, attention has to be paid to support prostheses. There are numerous cases of loss of limbs due to the conflict, mines, and the earthquake. Water and sanitation systems also need considerable improvement. Veterinary vaccines are needed for maintaining the livestock in the country.

Refugees and internally displaced persons are in dire need of a variety of assistance which ranges from the provision of shelters to protection and non-food assistance. Public and community buildings are still occupied by refugees across the country.

The Armenian government needs help in building up its capacity to effectively coordinate and channel humanitarian assistance. This is required in the form of a consolidation of various governmental agencies dealing with aid and in the establishment of an adequate data processing network.

In Armenia it is extremely difficult to assess accurate population figures. A large number of Armenians have left the country for the economic zones of Russia and elsewhere in search of work because of the harsh economic situation in Armenia. However, most of them have left their family members behind. Especially in winter this results in the presence of a disproportionately large number of vulnerable groups, such as women, children, and pensioners. There are a total of 631,000 pensioners in Armenia, including 457,000 elderly pensioners. These vulnerable sections of the population survive by selling their belongings to supplement whatever remittances they receive from abroad. However most personal resources of this type have by this time been depleted. Therefore identification of vulnerable groups to include most needy refugees, displaced persons, pensioners, orphans, handicapped and disabled persons, and children is critical. The government has made efforts to do this systematically by building up a data bank of vulnerable families under its program, the first phase of which, involving voluntary registration, is complete; 600,000 families have been registered as needing assistance, of which 150,000 families were identified by the government as most needy.

Now let me draw your attention to the main priorities in the development of Technical Assistance programs and the organizations performing them. Important technical assistance programs have been performed by the European Union (EU), USAID, UNDP, UNICEF, UNHCR,, World Bank, IMF, IOM, and by different countries according to their program agreements. One of the biggest and important technical assistance programs is the Tacis program, which has sound ties with the different NIS republics. In 1991 the European Union Board provided Armenia 2.77 million ecus for national development programs only. Besides the national programs, Armenia has also parrot regional programs, where in 1992 9 million ecus was spent. In 1993/94 the budget for technical assistance was 9 million ecus. The significant part of the budget is spent on the trips and salaries of qualified specialists; 10 percent is spent on providing new technology and training specialists'.

Since the beginning of the implementation of the main directions of the program, it was decided to focus attention on the following areas: energy, transportation, the banking system, agriculture, food production, and the training of specialists. Currently the most important areas to be strengthened are energy, privatization programs in industry, and capacity building projects.

I would like to emphasize that one of the important parts of all the technical assistance projects is preparation of highly qualified specialist. As you probably know, Armenia was one of the republics of the former Soviet Union with a highly qualified labor force and intellectual potential. This tendency remains nowadays. However, in order to facilitate transition to an open, market-oriented economy, it is imperative for our government to reeducate specialists. In this regard it has become important to engage specialists from the different branches of the economy under the programs of technical assistance. We have obtained certain positive results in this area. For instance, numerous training courses were organized in the United States, France, Germany, Japan, and Italy for our economists, lawyers, doctors, agricultural specialists, and managers from public and private organizations during the last two to three years.

Having analyzed our experiences and mistakes related to the procedures for selection of our nominees, we have designed a precise framework for appropriate options for specialists. Pursuant to the government's resolution, the Ministry of the Economy is responsible for management and coordination of all assistance flows, particularly for technical assistance. Based on the main priorities of development identified by the government, taking into account the requests from the different ministries and organizations, a proposal on training has been drawn up. After adoption of the above-mentioned proposal, it has to be submitted to the international organizations and to the separate countries for their consideration and final approval.

Now let me present the order of adequate selection of specialists. Initially ministries and organizations have presented their nominees to the Aid Coordination Department of the Ministry of Economy. Then, sponsoring international organizations with the Ministry of the Economy review their application forms and make final decisions. I would like to emphasize that one of the main points of selection is the presence of 40 percent of women in the groups to be trained.

Currently, two large-scale organizations (IMF, USAID) have accomplished the largest training programs in Armenia. Nowadays, the NGO Training Center has started to operate within the framework of USAID. The main objectives of this center are the provision of updated information to specialists from the different non-governmental organizations in order to facilitate their contacts with the donor community.

The New Economic Climate in Armenia

Kohar Yenokian*

I congratulate you, members and participants of AIWA's First International Conference. I also express my deep gratitude to the organizers, who made the idea of women's equality with men—in every aspect of life, as well as the protection of women's rights and creating new opportunities for them—the thesis statement of this conference. It is a great honor for the Armenian people to know that successes and problems are being addressed in this beautiful hall. The Armenian nation, known for its rich history and culture, became particularly well-known after the devastating earthquake which left us in a harsh social and economic condition. However all peoples of the world, the English included, stretched out their hands to provide Armenia with humanitarian aid. Our deep gratitude goes to them for such a noble attitude.

The only way out of the grave situation resulting from the earthquake was to organize work in all directions. We were at the same time dependent solely upon the offered help, a situation which eventually could have disgraced our nation and defamed its long-suffering and creative people. It would have killed diligence, making our nation incapable of working. To make my point concrete, let me recall a French parable.

Kohar Yenokian is director of the Garoun Garment Factories in Armenia.

To help a needy neighbor with milk for her son, a wealthy individual begins to give some milk to the poor family every day. This continues until one day the wealthy woman gets tired. She stops giving milk, but instead buys a cow for her neighbor. The poor neighbor now has her own milk supply by taking care of her cow.

I would like to draw a conclusion: it would be fantastic if the help we are receiving consisted in finding a mechanism which would bring us out of our unfavorable economic situation.

At this moment, the Armenian woman does not have the opportunity to work. Therefore she is deprived of her rights, because only in work are the abilities and creative powers of the individual realized. In spite of the fact there is no legal distinction in Armenia between the rights of men and women, the participation of women in the work of the Parliament and Government is hardly comparable to that of the women of progressive countries. The Armenian woman is saddled with the bulk of family duties, thus finding herself in a grim social condition. The harshest is the situation of single mothers, as well as those with many children, who are unable to provide their children with adequate daily food and clothing.

Women at the "Garoun" factories of which I am the director are also in a difficult situation. Eighty percent of the personnel consists of women. To create an adequate idea of the organization of work, it may be useful to cast a retrospective glance at the situation in Soviet times. Our economy then was planned. According to previously made agreements with Russia, resources and additional materials were shipped to us at a very low cost, with no transportation problem existing whatsoever. Our production was then sent to all of the Republics of the Soviet Union as well as, of course, to commercial organizations in Armenia—in accordance with demand.

Armenia is now independent, and so are the former republics of the USSR. Every one of them ordered its own will and created its own currency. All of the former banking operations were liquidated, and it became impossible to solve any question by means of a financial transfer. The war, which is going on for the sixth year now, brought forth its hardships, too.

Armenia is in an economic crisis. Raw materials have gone up in cost several times. All roads are blocked, and the only possible transport is aerial, which is five times more expensive for an enterprise. The structure of labor organization has collapsed, and the enterprises are sinking. The accumulated resources have become exhausted, which has resulted in the stoppage of work, which in turn brought unemployment to thousands of workers, who thus lost their tiny salaries.

At the "Garoun" factories we had to find a way to return to work as it had been conducted before. And we found it by applying a form of Eastern work scheme, i.e. providing labor in return for raw and supplementary materials and shipping the production afterwards to the West for appropriate payment. Only when the blockade is over, the roads reopened, and the banking problems resolved will it be possible for us to find the materials we need and to send the production to any country.

Many businessmen have come and still are coming to Armenia. It seemed that they were all willing to cooperate with us, they would suggest projects, but as soon as we began to discuss questions of raw materials and transportation, the wartime situation involuntarily became an impediment, and hence the mere signing of a protocol would be postponed for at least two years. And our factory continued to remain in an awful situation. At last a door of opportunity opened for us. In an Armenian family of seven living in Holland, three of five sons expressed a wish to work with Armenia in spite of their realistic knowledge of the current situation. Ignoring all problems, they signed a contract with "Garoun" for three years. According to its terms, they were to supply us with raw and auxiliary materials after which they would transport the production to Holland by air. This was very a positive arrangement, on one hand, because in this way our production would appear in stores in Holland in no time at all; however, on the other hand, flight expenses were quite high. Today ours is almost the only enterprise in operation out of all light industry in Armenia.

Thanks to the Armenian family of Keleji from Almelo, Holland, our employees were able to return to work, thus reviving the pulse of the rhythm that gives rise to hope for a brighter future and bringing us out of the lengthy period of stress.

But just think how many enterprises are stalled! I would like to appeal to all of you: when you go back to your countries, please find active businessmen who work in the field of light industry. Let them not turn to Algeria, Tunisia, Hong Kong, Taiwan, Morocco, or other countries in search of labor markets. Let them consider Armenia to help her in organizing and providing people with jobs without interruption.

We know that the United Nations Women's Conference in Beijing in 1995 will follow the present forum. Please, help us solve our problems, so that in Beijing we may address more serious issues, without specially emphasizing hardships in the social and economic aspects of our lives.

I invite all the organizers and participants to visit our beautiful Armenia. Upon witnessing in person the marvel of our nation, you will realize how you can contribute to the reconstruction of our economy with new technology, sophisticated techniques, and the latest developments in the field.

(Translated by Anahit Tovmassian Shahinian)

How to Influence the Political Process

Rita Balian*

The general theme of this session is how to further the Armenian agenda through political and cultural activities. While this agenda is not gender-specific, Armenian women have played and continue to play a vital role in linking the promotion of Armenian culture with the advancement of political policy. I will give some background information and discuss some lessons learned from my experiences over many years in this field.

OUTLINE:
I. What is the Political Process and Why Influence It
II. Traditional Lobbying
III. Non-traditional Lobbying
IV. Some General Pointers
V. Some Lessons Learned
VI. Conclusion

WHAT IS THE POLITICAL PROCESS AND WHY INFLUENCE IT

With the fall of the Soviet Union and the birth of the independent Republic of Armenia, the challenges facing the Armenian nation today have increased manyfold. The success

---

Rita Balian has been active in community activities in the United States and Armenia. She played a major role in establishing the sister-city relationship between Alexandria, Virgina, and Giumri, Armenia,

or failure of this new democracy rests not only in the hands
of the Armenians in Armenia, but also in the hands of the
millions of Armenians in the diaspora. Our ability as Armenians, and more importantly as Americans, Canadians, and
Europeans, among others, to influence the political process in
our respective countries is vital to the survival of Armenia.
In today's global, political, and economic environments,
decisions made in Washington, London, Paris, Bonn, and
Tokyo affect the lives of millions around the world. We no
longer have the luxury of relying on the political skills of
others, and thus must work to further develop our own
political acumen. Influencing the political process is a
complex and challenging effort that requires both institutional and individual involvement. As individual volunteers
we can make efforts to influence the decision-makers in the
political process; however, in order to be truly effective, we
must first define and understand the process itself.

Most of us live in some form of a representative democracy, whether it is parliamentary (Great Britain), presidential (United States and France), or a combination thereof. A
democracy is a way of governing in which the whole body of
citizens takes charge of its own affairs. The word "democracy"
derives from two Greek words: *demos,* meaning "the people,"
and *kratos,* meaning "rule," which combined means "the rule
of the people." A true democracy, as the fifteenth president of
the United States, Abraham Lincoln, defined it, requires "a
society in which all the people are citizens with the same
rights to participate in government." This means that the
individual citizens or groups of citizens have as much access
to their representatives as any large or wealthy group. As a
citizen of the United States of America, I am most familiar
with the American political process and will refer to examples within this framework. However, the basic lessons
learned from the American experience can be applied to other
parts of the world because, while the means of forming a

democracy have been different throughout the world, the end purpose is the same.

The most direct way of exercising influence in government is to elect Armenians to public office. This can be accomplished in three ways. The first way is by having a significant number of Armenian voters; the second, by having the financial resources to run well-organized and effective campaigns; and the third, by relying on a combination of the two. While having large communities in California, Massachusetts, and New York, Armenians in the United States are not a large enough voting block to single-handedly elect Armenians to office. We must rely on the support of others. As a result our ability to raise funds within the community becomes more crucial. Examples of this are the fund-raising efforts of the Armenians in helping launch the campaigns of former Governor George Deukmejian and former Congressman Charles ("Chip") Pashayan, both from California, and the current campaign of Chuck Haytaian, the Republican nominee to the U.S. Senate from New Jersey. While our fund-raising abilities are respectable, they are modest when compared with the resources available to other larger groups. Therefore it is essential that Armenians not only seek public office, but also work actively in the campaigns of other representatives and senators to establish credibility and thus gain influence in the decision-making process. This form of influence is more indirect in its approach, but can be equally as effective in its outcome.

TRADITIONAL LOBBYING

The process of participating in government by influencing the decision-makers who affect how government performs is what we call lobbying. The term derives from the fact that historically attempts to put pressure on legislators often took place in the lobby or vestibule adjacent to the legislative chamber. In the United States this activity is most commonly associated with private interest groups, such as large organizations, corporations, or labor unions; however, it also can be carried out by individuals. Lobbying may be done openly before legislative committees or administrative forums, and it may also be accomplished through private meetings with public officials to address specific concerns. Some organizations lobby through grass-roots campaigns, which mobilize the membership to actively pursue a goal that usually attracts the media and thus builds support for their cause.

Most democratic governments are composed of competing interest groups and factions. In the United States these factions are controlled for the most part by a system of checks and balances that is established by our Constitution, which divides our government into three branches: the legislative, executive, and judicial. Each branch plays a part in the decision-making process. Citizens lobby the executive and legislative branches of government because elected officials owe service to the people who live in their districts and states. Politicians who blatantly disregard their constituents are usually, but not always, defeated in the next election.

There are quite a number of powerful lobby groups in the United States. Some of the big players are the associations representing large industries like the oil companies and auto makers, and the associations representing specific groups like the American Association of Retired Persons, the American Medical Association, the National Rifle Association, and the National Organization of Women. A voice for the Armenians in the nation's capital is the Armenian Assembly of America. Founded in 1976, the Assembly serves as an organization that conducts formal lobbying for Armenia and Armenian causes. They educate congressmen and senators about issues concerning Armenia and cultivate the political will necessary to push through legislation that is favorable to Armenian interests. Sonia Messerian Crow, an attorney and a former Reagan Administration official, recently served as the Assembly's Director for Government Affairs. She did an exceptional job in leading the effort for pro-Armenia legislation in the U.S. Congress. Likewise in Armenia, the former Assembly representative, Gassia Apkarian, another attorney, organized and managed visits of American political figures to Armenia in a way that further promoted Armenian interests. These important visits showed the representatives and senators the difficult conditions under which the Armenian people live, and thus convinced them to approve more humanitarian aid. Ever since the 1988 earthquake in Armenia, the Assembly has employed an effective lobbying tool called the Action Alert. An Action Alert is issued about a specific issue or event of concern to Armenians and sent throughout the nation to mobilize the communities to notify their representatives and tell them of the importance of this specific issue or event to the community. A recent example was the successful effort to attain a $75 million aid package for Armenia. Currently, the Assembly is working on securing passage of the Humanitarian Aid Corridor Act.

Two and a half years ago, in February 1992, a small group of individuals, led by Nancy Najarian from Boston, Massachusetts, formed the American Committee to Lift the Blockade of Armenia. This nonpartisan committee began as a local group and mushroomed into a nationwide campaign. An example of a grass-roots movement, the committee organized a letter-writing campaign that sent thousands of telegrams and petitions to the White House, Congress, and the United Nations. Through letters, phone calls, demonstrations, and marches, Armenians throughout America made their representatives and the general public aware of the harsh winter conditions in Armenia. As a result the campaign not only raised the awareness of the media and the public, but also was crucial in securing emergency shipments of heating oil and kerosine lanterns.

Recently, the Armenian-American community has grown even more politically sophisticated by becoming involved in the political campaigns of a number of prominent Senators and Representatives who, as a result, have become our advocates. By giving money, volunteering our time, and getting our communities out to vote for these candidates, we have established the credibility necessary to request political favors.

All of the above are examples of traditional straight-forward lobbying, where the actions of a group of citizens directly influence the formation of public policy. However, there exists a non-traditional way that is more subtle in its approach, but equally successful in establishing the foundation for direct access to decision-makers. This foundation serves as the basis for my ability as an individual to influence policy-makers and facilitate the more formal lobbying efforts of groups like the Assembly.

NON-TRADITIONAL LOBBYING

Before the earthquake of 1988 and the independence of Armenia in 1991, Armenian organizations in America focused primarily on issues related to the genocide, especially obtaining recognition of its occurrence from the American and Turkish governments. While receiving such recognition was important, the need to attract Armenian-American youth back to their communities and make them proud of their heritage was equally as important. As it has been stated many times, the youth are our future: they will be the leaders of tomorrow, whether in politics, journalism, academics, art, business, law, or medicine. Our efforts in assisting them along this path will lay the foundation and serve as an investment for the future. If they have benefited from the efforts of the community, they will be more likely to become our advocates when they attain leadership positions.

One way of realizing this goal was to organize high caliber events that catered not only to the Armenian community, but also, and more importantly, to the American public. As chairperson of the Washington, D.C., Chapter of the Armenian General Benevolent Union for eight years (from 1980 to 1988), I involved the youth in assisting in the organization of civic and cultural activities that showcased the best in Armenian talent to the nation's capital. These events, while not always political in nature, served as a means of indirect lobbying by attracting important politicians, prominent Washingtonians, and the media; consequently, they kept Armenians in the minds of others.

Some of these events and tributes honored William Saroyan at the National Press Club, Metropolitan Opera Stars Lili Chookasian and Ara Berberian at the Kennedy Center with Maestro Mstislav Rostropovich, world-renowned violist Kim Kashkashian and Tokyo String Quartet First Violinist Peter Oundjian at the Corcoran Art Gallery, and the Chopin International Piano Competition winner Arthur Papazian and composer Alan Hovhaness at the prestigious National Departmental Auditorium. We established a "Youth Leadership Development Group" that functioned as a core group of young people who would be involved in different aspects of organizing various projects. This kept the youth together and provided opportunities for them to be a part of the influential cultural life in Washington.

As examples I would like to highlight and discuss three projects in detail. The first is an on-going program whose focus is on our youth, and the other two are recent events that produced positive feedback.

In 1987, with the funds raised from the AGBU President's Club, I, along with my husband, initiated the AGBU New York Summer Internship Program and in 1989, the Los Angeles Summer Internship Program. These programs provide Armenian college and graduate students with an opportunity to gain valuable professional experience through summer internships and also foster an increased awareness of their Armenian heritage through extra-curricular activities. In its eighth year, the AGBU internship programs have had over three hundred alumni, and this year thirty-five interns from nine countries participated in the New York program alone. While bringing our youth together, these programs also give them the opportunity to meet, talk to, and often work with the decision-makers in their chosen fields. Along with the Armenian Assembly Internship Program in Washington, these programs are an invaluable investment in our future.

In 1989, shortly after the Earthquake in Armenia, I was moved by the life-changing experiences of the emergency rescue teams that had gone to Leninakan from Virginia, and I wanted to maintain and develop that relationship. As a result I lobbied then Mayor and current U.S. Congressman Jim Moran of the city of Alexandria, Virginia, a major suburb of Washington, to form a sister-city relationship with Leninakan (now known as Giumri) Armenia. He agreed. Since its inception in 1989, we have educated many citizens of Alexandria about Giumri and the people and culture of Armenia through numerous art, music, and social events. Many of our national politicians make their Washington home in Alexandria, and thus we have exposed them to the existence and importance of our nation. Also, we have gained in Jim Moran a very important ally in the U.S. Congress.

Recently, the Sister City Committee won a grant from the United States Information Agency (USIA) and Sister Cities International under the auspices of the "Freedom Support Act" to initiate a Thematic Youth Exchange. This exchange brought ten young Armenian music students from Giumri, Armenia, to Alexandria, Virginia, in April 1994. The theme for the exchange was "Linking the Two Cities Through the Arts." During their three-week stay in America, the students performed a number of concerts as a gesture of gratitude to the American public and the U.S. government agencies for their humanitarian, technical, and financial assistance after the 1988 earthquake. The concerts were held at the World Bank (which last year authorized $28 million for the reconstruction effort of the earthquake zone), the U.S. Information Agency/Voice of America (VOA), the U.S. Department of Agriculture, the State Department (through the Agency for International Development), the Library of Congress, and the American Red Cross. The indirect benefit of these concerts was to expose the story of these children, who lived through the earthquake and live through the current problems of day-to-day life in Armenia to hundreds of Americans, especially political leaders, government officials, and journalists.

Many of these same government officials and politicians are currently working on issues affecting Armenia, such as government exchanges and assistance. We personalized their experience with Armenia by focusing on a group of children playing beautiful folk music. We sent a powerful message that will serve us well in future dealings with these individuals. The Sister City Program and the visit of the children was our "door opener." The uniqueness of the theme and our method of presentation—as a gesture of appreciation—was something no one could refuse. The quality and professionalism of our programs displayed the talent of Armenia's young citizens in a way that the attendees will not forget for some time to come.

In May of this year, Sonia Missirian Crow, Maggie Kamalian, and I, along with Dr. Donald Miller and Lorna Touryan Miller of Los Angeles, organized a reception and exhibition of photographs entitled "Armenia: Portraits of Survival." The photographs were displayed in the Rotunda of the U.S. Senate Russell and Dirksen Office Buildings, thus exposing members of the Senate and their staff to these moving photos. The staff members are as important, if not more so, than the senators and congressmen because they arrange the schedules, set the priorities, and research the subjects when helping the lawmakers with their decisions. Through this exhibition, we not only showcased the professional and well-prepared art work of photojournalist Jerry Berndt—work that movingly portrayed the agony and suffering in Armenia today—but we also were able to involve over a dozen Washington lawmakers who spoke on behalf of Armenia and pledged their continuing commitment to help alleviate the suffering shown in the photographs. The exhibition was a success; its purpose was to serve as a poignant reminder to the members of Congress of the continued suffering of the Armenian people through the harsh winters, war, and blockade.

These three examples represent different ways of accomplishing the same goal—raising awareness within the non-Armenian community of issues important to Armenians. However, before we can ask the support of public officials, we must first participate in their election campaigns, whether as volunteers or fund-raisers. We must first give so that we can call their attention to our needs and ask for their support in the future.

SOME GENERAL POINTERS

How does one go about raising awareness and exercising influence in the political process? The first step is to establish a specific goal—whether it is to lift the blockade, pass a bill, appropriate humanitarian aid, recognize a prominent Armenian, or further the careers of our youth. The second step is to learn as much as possible about how things work in the world you are entering. What are the protocols? What is the proper course of business? Who are the key people to approach? How do you attain the goals you are pursuing?

In finding the answers to these questions, do not be afraid to ask questions. If approached correctly, people will be flattered that you value their opinion and will go out of their way to help you. Learn the processes of the group you want to influence. As much as we might think we know, we can always learn from others.

An excellent way of gaining valuable insight is by becoming involved in American cultural and artistic organizations, such as galleries, children's museums, and local symphony orchestras. On these committees you will meet a variety of influential people who will form your network of friends and acquaintances. They will appreciate your involvement and will repay you with their support for your projects. More specifically and directly, volunteer to raise funds for congressional campaigns. You can begin by calling friends, Armenian and non-Armenian, for assistance, donations, and votes; then continue with direct fund-raising by hosting or sponsoring an event in your home.

Forming ad hoc committees will assist you in planning projects. These committees can be composed of individuals who can write well, who can prepare refreshments, who can act as hosts and hostesses, who can keep the project's financial books, who can use computers for preparing letters and mailing lists, and who can provide music and entertainment. They should all be willing to publicize the project, sell tickets, raise funds, and get others to help. In one word, your team should include people who are ready to put some time, effort and talent to make any project successful. Team effort is very important; therefore, it is crucial to select individuals who work well together and complement each other's skills.

Last year a group of talented individuals agreed to work with me and the Armenian Embassy in Washington to organize a Tribute Reception in honor of Charles Aznavour, Armenia's Ambassador-at-Large. Aznavour was in Washington performing with the very popular Liza Minelli. Taking hold of this opportunity, we planned a tribute to honor him for his humanitarian work on behalf of the people of Armenia. By including his good friend and associate Liza Minelli in the program, we guaranteed a large turnout from the community, especially government and public officials. We had over 350 guests on that day, of which thirty-five were high-level officials from the State Department, the White House, and the National Security Council, nineteen were Congressmen, and seven were Senators, including Bob Dole, who spoke very eloquently about his continuing commitment to help Armenia. An all-around team effort helped produce a very successful event in one of the city's finest hotels, it showcased the Armenian Embassy in a way that was comparable with large embassies and powerful lobby groups, and it raised close to $100,000 as a down payment for the new embassy building.

I cannot stress enough that all the work you do must be of the highest quality and must meet the highest standards. This standard is what makes it unique, what grabs the interest of the group, what keeps people coming back, and what they remember in conjunction with things that are Armenian. This reputation for excellence will be one of the factors that attracts decision-makers to choose your event over the many other invitations they receive. Since our economic resources and national media exposure are not as established as other groups, we must use our resources with intelligence, imagination, and flair. One successful tool that adds flair is catering with Armenian cuisine. This creates a truly unique setting that becomes more memorable. Another tool is having a celebrity attend the event. In both cases, people will remember their enjoyment more and will always respond positively in the future when they are invited, or when you call them for a political consideration. The basic lesson is that through our imagination we must creatively use every resource at our disposal to further our agenda.

SOME LESSONS LEARNED

I would like to share with you some of the lessons I have learned from my experiences:

- Good salesmanship is the essence of success.

- Know your "product" well because that is what you will be presenting or pursuing as a goal. You cannot educate others unless you are well informed yourself.

- Be convinced of the value of the product or the goal in order to convince others to join in helping and/or to accept the idea you are promoting.

- Marketing is important. You have to "dress up" your product in such a way to make it so that it will attract attention and achieve the results you want. The benefits that people receive must always be greater than what you are "charging" them.

- Strategic planning is vital. Plan on paper to determine strengths and weaknesses. Define your purpose and goal, and design your method of presentation to sell your idea accordingly.

- Always involve different groups, organizations, and individuals in the planning and preparations. However, first you should be totally involved before you expect others to get involved also.

- Be meticulous in your work and make sure your committee is also. Paperwork should be complete and organized; always follow-up with thank you letters and phone calls.

- Constantly review the quality of the work and always improve what you are doing. You get what you inspect, not what you expect.

and last, but most certainly not least,

- You must first give in order to receive.

CONCLUSION

In conclusion, as Armenians and as women, we are faced today with great challenges and even greater opportunities. The days of the exclusively male-dominated decision-making structures are becoming obsolete. Not only are women influencing the decision-makers today, but they are also becoming those decision-makers. Part of influencing the political process is empowering ourselves to take a more active part in it. More and more, women are playing a major part in planning and organizing significant events and projects. AIWA is a network of such women leaders.

By becoming involved, an individual develops and empowers herself. Whether you are shy or someone who gets involved for intellectual stimulation while you are at home with your children, you will develop self-confidence through your volunteer experiences. Your skills in working with people and making presentations and speeches will grow, and you will become a more accomplished person, which in turn will empower you to tackle more challenging obstacles. These are the means through which we can empower women and bring them into leadership roles. Through service, our young Armenian women will prepare themselves for their professional careers, their communities, and their families. This is what true empowerment is all about—individual women gaining the confidence and know-how to reach their true potential, whether it is in community service, family life, or professional work.

I am proud to tell you about a significant program of events we are planning for in 1998 in Washington. It consists of an exhibition of Armenian Manuscripts at the Library of Congress, a folk art exhibition from Armenia at the Smithsonian International Art Gallery Section, and an exhibit of art works by Reuben Nakian to commemorate his 100th anniversary at the American Museum of Art, the Corcoran Gallery, or the Hirshhorn Museum. It will be the Year of Armenian

Culture, and will have a big impact on the nation's capital.

While not political in nature, these exhibits will receive notable media coverage, and thus will attract the leaders and decision-makers in Washington. The manuscripts will show the world that Armenian culture is ancient and meaningful, the folk art will show that Armenians have cherished art and handiwork throughout the centuries, and the Nakian exhibit will reaffirm Nakian's significant contribution to developments in art in the twentieth century.

How to Develop Collaborative Programs

Nancy Sweezy*

I will read to you from an article of August 28, 1994, in the *Washington Post* by Paul Richard, a friend of mine, covering the opening in Baltimore of the ancient Armenian manuscript exhibition originated by the Morgan Library in New York:

> That the Armenians survive is something of a miracle. Just think of their enemies—Alexander's armies, the mighty Roman legions, the Persians, the Parthians, the Sassanids, the caliphs of Baghdad, Timur's Mongol hordes, the Turks, the Germans and the Russians. And they're fighting still, with Azerbaijian. As a people, as a culture, they've been beaten up so often they ought to be extinct. Their culture has sustained them.

> Armenian beliefs and values have been expressed over the centuries through many art forms. The best known in the outside world are the illuminated manuscripts that Paul Richard wrote about, medieval church architecture, and woven rugs. There is, however, a wide range of other arts of high quality and significance to be considered, and when the traditional arts are taken altogether, they tell the story of Armenian culture.

Nancy Sweezy is a folklorist and director of Country Roads, a non-profit organization engaged in cultural conservation projects.

In 1988 I visited Armenia for the first time on a Cambridge-Yerevan Sister City trip. I am a folklorist and, as always, I was looking for folk art. I found it at the Museum of Folk Art in Yerevan. I was struck by the quality of the museum's collections and surprised to learn that a large number of artisans were still at work making lace, embroidering, and carving wood. I learned that only a few of their artifacts had been shown abroad, and the museum's director and I agreed to try to bring a show to the United States. In 1990 I returned and a collaboration began. It took me two years to convince Professor Levon Abrahamian to take the time in his busy schedule to work with us on a book. But when he did agree and gathered together a group of scholars, the doors began to open more completely for the book and also for the exhibition.

Our collaboration has become the Armenia Cultural Project of Country Roads, Inc., a twenty-eight-year-old, non-profit, cultural conservation foundation. In this project we have undertaken to produce an exhibition and a book about Armenian culture and, as a corollary, to organize forums for discussion of current cultural issues facing Armenia and other newly independent Republics of the former Soviet Union.

The exhibition will present the material and mythic culture of Armenia as it developed over millennia in the highlands south of the Caucasus Mountains and, until early in this century, on the Anatolian plateau of present-day Turkey. It will focus on the values and beliefs of the Armenian people as seen in their arts, architecture, and other cultural expressions that they have sustained, and in turn been sustained by, over a long and rich history. It will include artifacts made of clay, metal, fabric, wood, and stone, and also photographs of various sizes (some very large) to bring the visitor a sense of place and people. Other media available for viewing and listening within the exhibition and available for purchase in the museum shops will include films, videotapes of rituals, ceremonies, crafting processes, and audio tapes of liturgical and other traditional music.

A series of satellite programs will accompany the exhibition, such as:

—music and dance programs by Armenian-American performing groups and, if feasible, by groups from Armenia;

—craft demonstrations by local artisans and possible some from Armenia;

—educational events pertaining to Armenian culture, such as teacher's workshops (with resource materials); hands-on programs for children;

—films, such as those directed by Sergei Parajanov.

The Armenia Cultural Project has located and documented Armenian-American artisans and performing artists who show keen interest in participating in the exhibition and its satellite programs.

The forums would be developed in collaboration with scholars, artists, and cultural conservators in both Armenia and the United States and would take place during exhibition showings. As perceived now, they would take as their subject current and evolving issues related to the interplay of commerce and culture in Armenia.

The book, which will consist of essays on various aspects of Armenian traditional culture, is being written by ethnographers, anthropologists, and ethnomusicologists in Armenia. It will be written in accessible prose, extensively illustrated, and published by University of Indiana Press in 1997.

The final component of the project is an export marketing program for Armenian handcrafts. The Armenia Cultural Project began to market these crafts in 1992 and, with help from Aid to Artisans in Connecticut, has offered a selection of crafts at three International Gift Fairs in New York with growing success. Last month a $7,000 order of embroidered place mats and napkins with matching carved wooden napkin rings was placed with Armenian Crafts, USA, Inc., by Nieman Marcus. In the co-op being set up in Yerevan there is an increasing emphasis on women's fabric art. Apparently this is happening because women see this as a clear opportunity to use their skills productively for economic gain, while men (and this is conjecture) may be dreaming of bigger and quicker success. The women, of course, are right to plunge in and begin to build on what they already have.

We believe that, by articulating Armenia's most enduring values as expressed in their arts, the exhibition and its accompanying programs can have a positive effect in these times of dislocation and stress. We also believe that this is an optimal time for such presentations for several reasons:

1) interest has surfaced in the United States about the cultures hidden for nearly a century within the eastern bloc;

2) the material we will exhibit has not been seen in the West;

3) the exhibition will draw attention to the rich culture of Armenia, enabling Armenians (and maybe others) to see beyond their perception of Armenians as "victims";

4) the exhibition will bring to diasporan Armenians aspects of their cultural roots about which second and third generation individuals have little knowledge;

5) the connection with outside museums will benefit the participating Armenian museums;

6) the exhibition and its satellite programs will reaffirm for all Armenians their identity as a people of gifted expression;

7) there is considerable interest in the exhibition both in Armenia and in America.

The project has already raised 68 percent of the funds needed to complete the preparatory work and has a commitment to cover transportation of the exhibition materials, which amounts to between 10 and 15 percent of the direct exhibition costs which are estimated at a minimum of

$275,000. We have done well in obtaining the commitment of substantial funding, but of course a considerable amount must still be raised.

Overall the project is very exciting and challenging, and we are aware that we cannot accomplish it by ourselves. I address you because I know that it is you, the Armenian women, wherever you live, who can work with us in the final years to bring these ambitious cultural programs to fruition. Furthermore, there lies before us all the possibility of creating the year-long celebration of Armenian culture proposed for 1998.

In closing, I particularly draw to your attention the fact that Armenian women are involved in all aspects of this collaborative project, both in Armenia and in America, as fabric artists, scholars, organizers, and supporters. Will you join us in celebrating Armenian culture?

Career Strategies for Young Professional Women

Nora A. Janoyan*

Young professional Armenian women are faced with the challenges of leading our people into the twenty-first century. In our diasporan communities as well as Armenia, Armenian women have moved graciously and with confidence into the professional arena. This conference is living proof of how far we've come as Armenian women.

At this session we will discuss a few key issues that will help young professionals in their career strategies. The session will be divided into four distinct areas.

1. Self Assessment and Development
2. Building a "Network"
3. Defining Your Ethnicity
4. The Personal Perspective

SELF ASSESSMENT

1. Self assessment is the inventory you conduct to determine your personal traits and skills.

2. This process of identifying your individual abilities, qualities, needs, and attributes is essential, first in order to determine your marketability in the work force and more importantly to define what you want to do with your life.

Nora A. Janoyan is senior financial analyst for Paramount Pictures in Los Angeles.

Under the category of abilities and skills there are three types of skills that you should identify.

Functional Skills - reflect your talents and aptitude both natural and developed such as managing, organizing, and coordinating skills. In this category practice makes perfect!!

Adaptive Skills - are developed from life experiences such as flexibility, leadership, patience, independence, decisiveness. These are adjustment skills that are crucial in the working environment.

Work-Content Skills - are learned skills related to your job such as being an intern or going through a training program.

3. After identifying your skills, it is just as important to assess your overall presence, attitude, and behavior.

4. Presence constitutes your appearance and manners. Dress professionally (preferably on the conservative side) because first impressions can facilitate further consideration. Pay attention to the colors, your makeup, hair, and overall look.

5. Be prepared to answer questions with confidence in order to reflect firmness and stability.

6. Attitude and Behavior—Behavior is triggered by a stimulus—make sure you can control it. It is results oriented and usually the outcome of a situation. Attitude is a state of mind which can be controlled by your own internal being.

THE ART OF MAKING CONTACTS—NETWORKING

1. Networking is the most effective way to be "noticed" by your surroundings.

2. With thought, sensitivity, and preparation, networking can become a natural way to build productive relationships that could enhance your career.

3. It is the best method of identifying the decision-makers and finding the means to reach them.

4. In the business world the strength of your network is determined by your "Rolodex power." At any given time you should be able to pull out your rolodex and with a bit of effort reach your professional goal.

5. Don't be bogged down by the "I'm nobody; therefore I don't know anyone important" blues.

6. Mobilize yourself and take advantage of the contacts that you possess, because they provide the vital link between you and the people you are trying to meet.

7. Never underestimate the value of any person you know.

8. Curiosity opens most unexpected doors—be straightforward and get in the habit of asking anyone and everyone what they do and whom they know in the field.

9. Keep your ears open and be informed about the situations around you.

10. There is no such thing as a person who cannot be contacted.

11. Business relationships function on the exchange of favors and information; therefore, recognize that the person being approached has as much to gain as you.

12. There is always an element of "luck" that is beyond your control, but the question is: "How can you best organize your luck, so the factors that are within your control are working for you?"

13. Many people who call themselves "lucky" are the ones who unconsciously refine their ability to learn about things as quickly as they happen and have developed the habit of putting themselves in touch with the right ears.

14. Once you've established and created a contact with a key individual, make sure you nourish and personalize the relationship in order to keep the information line flowing.

15. Remember that people are connected to one another

by nearly infinite number of pathways. Many of these pathways are available to you, but you must activate the circuits to make them work to your advantage.

I want to share the findings of a research study done in Boston to illustrate the extraordinary power of using personal contacts. The research study called "Small World Problem" reveals that on an average a person of adult age will accumulate 500 to 1,000 personal contacts. Professor Stanley Milgram reasons that each link between two individuals generates a total pool of contacts numbering between 250,000 (500 x 500) to 1 million. Three links in the referral chain permits an astronomical number of contact possibilities. Therefore, he reasons that anyone ought to be able to reach anyone else in a populated country simply by putting a few links of referral chains into operation. The results from testing this theory showed that people can typically reach their targeted individual within two links.

Reaching your professional goals can be very much enhanced by a bit of networking. Before the end of this conference you will all see how powerful this social tool is in reaching your professional and personal goals.

DEFINING YOUR ETHNICITY

1. The famous anthropologist Arnold Rose states that the Marginal Man moves out of his ethnic society until he is established. This concept is very internal and personal. The individual moves back into the ethnic community once he's made it in his profession, Charles Aznavour, Cher, Kirk Krikorian.

2. There is an extra endorsement and validity in your qualification once you come from a confirmed institution. The community will respect and honor you more.

3. You must remember that there is always room to "come back" into the community.

4. Presently there is a sociological paradigm in the

United States that is based on "Cultural Plurality." This philosophy of thought states that at first everyone was White Anglo-Saxon. Then we adopted the reality of a "melting pot," and now we've realized that each group has something to offer and is original in its own way. The perfect example is a symphony, where every instrument is needed to make music. Every single sound is needed to create harmonious totality.

5. Cultural Plurality can be easily applied to the recent existence of Armenian women worldwide. Each one of us coming from a different area of the world can contribute to the development and enhancement of Armenian women living in Armenia.

The following workshop participants will discuss "The Personal Perspective: A Quest for Excellence."

Allison Ann Arabian, Attorney at Law
Annie Kanzabedian, Hospital Administrator, RN
Zara Ingilizian, Associate Product Manager
Lisa Stepanian, Chemist
Linda Kay Abdulian, Educator

Nationalism and the Development of the Armenian Women's Rights Movement

Sona Zeitlian*

HISTORICAL PERSPECTIVE OF ARMENIAN WOMEN'S RIGHTS
Personal and Family Status Law

The first Armenian Book of Law, written by the monk Mekhitar Gosh, specifies that men and women had equal rights and were equally responsible for the welfare of the family. Men and women were free in their own spheres of activities—men as family providers and protectors, women as household and family organizers as well as transmitters of customs, traditions, moral values and national aspirations. During men's prolonged absences, women assumed the added roles of breadwinner and protector of the families.

Family law did not allow for such individual rights of a parent as the pursuit of happiness. Individual considerations disruptive of the family stability had to be sacrificed to uphold the paramount interests of the children and their right of family support.

The family structure was considered to be vital for the survival of the Armenians, a nation without the benefit of a strong central authority and frequently beset by enemies as well as wandering and plundering tribes.

Sona Zeitlian is the author of Armenian Women in the Revolutionary Movement *(Los Angeles, 1992, in Armenian).*

Early Christian Thought and the Status of the Armenian Woman

In spite of being spiritually equal, the Christian Church considered a woman's domain to be her home and family and her salvation from Eve's original sin to be prayer and abstinence.

On the other hand, the Armenian Apostolic church being an essentially national institution, Armenian women did not pursue a narrow life of personal salvation, but rather dedicated themselves to the national welfare and readily sacrificed themselves to uphold the faith of the nation. The concept of family, nation and church were inseparable. Hence, Armenian women had an active role in preserving the heritage of the Church as a national institution, especially during religious persecutions.

Roman Law and Armenian Women's Equal Property and Education Rights

During feudal times, Armenian women did not have property rights. Family or clan property was the indivisible wealth of male kinship.

During the Roman rule of Armenia, Emperor Justinian initiated equal property rights with the intention of weakening the influence of the landed gentry. He also initiated equal rights of education for the daughters of the gentry only.

Status of Armenian Women During Ottoman Rule Until Nineteenth Century

During almost six decades of Ottoman subjugation, Turkish culture made inroads mostly in such regions where Armenians, Turks and Kurds lived in close proximity. But in exclusively Armenian regions, such as Taron, Zeitun, Vaspuragan or Karabagh, the old traditions persisted.

In general, Armenian men and women did not have equal rights any longer. In rural areas of Western or Turkish

Armenia, girls were illiterate and their moral education consisted of religious precepts and superstitions. They began agricultural work at an early age, were married soon after puberty, then the obligatory mouthpiece became the symbol of their total obedience to the patriarch and members of the husband's extended family.

The subservient woman could be abused or beaten at will, even expelled, without anyone attempting to defend her. As the village life chronicler Telgadintsi (Hovhannes Harutunian, 1860-1915) reports, in some areas a man could even have two wives and the women would never dare to complain. Such treatment of women generated devious character traits, such as cunning, greediness, and underhanded behavior. Women's chief weapon was cursing, and the most pernicious curses were uttered by women.

Only motherhood had a liberating effect on women. Maternal love gushed freely, purified a woman's heart of all traces of bitterness, gave her authority in the family, instilled fierce family loyalty and the incentive to sacrifice personal advantage for the greater value of family solidarity. Consequently, only the sacred mother on whom the well being of the family and the survival of the nation depended was worthy of her people's and her nation's respect, even veneration.

Armenian society was not only patriarchal but patrilineal as well, tracing the relationships through the male line only. Male superiority was reinforced not only within the family unit but on a larger societal level, as the headman of the village was chosen by the patriarchs of the larger families.[1]

On the other hand, such urban centers as Constantinople and Smyrna enjoyed a cosmopolitan atmosphere. After 1790

---

[1]Susie Hoogasian and Mary Kilbourne-Matossian, *Armenian Village Life Before 1914* (Detroit, 1982), pp. 22-29.

the Ottoman government allowed the religious minorities (millet) to open communal schools. Yet the patriarchal culture upheld the superiority of the male, and whatever gains were achieved in terms of education or employment were negated by a communal moral code of behavior that repressed any significant role for women.

Eastern Armenia (annexed by the Russian Empire in the late 1820s) enjoyed better social and security conditions. Women took advantage of the social mobility to seek educational and employment opportunities. Yet the Armenian peasantry (upward of 80 percent) was backward and lived in poverty, with the extended family as the principle productive unit. On the other hand, the urban culture of Tbilisi and Baku was cosmopolitan.

In both the Turkish and Russian cosmopolitan centers, even the Armenian language had ceased to be a unifying factor and native Armenians conversed in Turkish, French, Russian, Georgian, even Circassian, whereas in rural Western Armenia there was a multiplicity of native dialects. In both the Turkish and Russian sectors socio-economic and cultural differences limited the communication of urban and rural Armenians and the sense of one nation and nationalist pride had to await the sweeping movements of modernization and national revival.

MODERNIZATION AND NATIONAL REVIVAL—THE DECLARATION OF ARMENIAN WOMEN'S RIGHTS

In both Western and Eastern Armenia, family and religion had defined the Armenians as a separate ethno-religious community. However, in the last decades of the nineteenth century both Western and Eastern Armenian youths made contact with the intellectual and political trends of Europe in Russian, German, Italian and French universities. This engendered a concentrated wave of intellectual and cultural energy which awakened national and political consciousness. The youths returned home with a national agenda of revival and advancement. The age-old Armenian pattern of seeking and assimilating international achievements to enrich and strengthen the national identity and the national heritage was at work once again.

The Declaration of Armenian Women's Rights

Women representatives of the nationalist intelligentsia such as the widely read writers Serpouhi Vahanian-Dussap and Zabel Assadour (Sybil) were genuine moral forces who led the women's rights movements with the following stipulations:

a.   Equal rights for men and women.

b.   Equal rights to choose a career and gainful employment.

c.   Removal from married life all double standards in favor of men.

d.   Right of women to higher learning as an essential means of improving child rearing and instruction as well as raising the standard of social interaction.

e.   Right of women to participate in the social sphere or equal role in the community.

f.   Elimination of the degrading customs of dowry, "head money," financial inducements, or benefits as a basis of marriage.

g.   Respect for ethnic values and traditions and at the same time acceptance of a modern liberal education that could enhance and strengthen the national identity and develop civic consciousness.

h.   Communication of women through the diffusion of ethnic culture, mobilization for self defense, and willingness to sacrifice for the national honor.

This declaration of Armenian women's rights is far from being a feminist push for liberation from the straits of patriarchal repression. The women intellectuals of the turn of the century were more intent on engaging women to being about social change and political reform. The rights of women went hand in hand with their obligations to strengthen the family structure and reinforce the survival of the nation.

Yet even a mild declaration of principles caused a great uproar, and such respected figures as the writer, jurist and member of parliament, Krikor Zohrab, doubted the need for equal rights when men and women were intended by nature to perform different tasks.

As a matter of fact, the crucial factor in any consideration of Armenian women's rights is the following. Armenia was a nation state for short periods only. Most of the time the land of the Armenians was divided and the nation subjugated and dispersed. This created a situation wherein the family assumed the unique role of assuring protection and survival as a nation. In such a situation, it is the woman's role in the family which becomes all important, and gender issues or inequalities are rarely subjected to open debate. Even in cases of open discrimination against women, equal justice has been subordinated to preserving the solidarity for men and the cohesion of the community.

Only the tide of nationalism at the turn of the century would have a direct impact on traditional conceptions.

IMPACT OF THE TIDE OF NATIONALISM ON THE WOMEN'S RIGHTS MOVEMENT

Role of Women During the Resistance

The massacres of 1895, the failure of reforms, arbitrary seizures and persecution in Western Armenia, the occupation of the national church and schools and various discriminatory practices in Eastern Armenia aroused the nationalist intelligentsia to organize an active resistance. They felt that their very survival as a nation was at stake.

The rising tide of nationalism gave women political identity and social status. They joined newly formed political organizations, took active part in the national mobilization, and distinguished themselves in the public sphere.

a. Education

Teaching was one of the few occupations in the Ottoman Empire open to women. Armenian women made most of this opportunity by spreading ethnic culture and the Armenian language as a potent symbol of national unity. They raised funds and established girls' schools in the backward provinces of Western Armenia to arouse awareness of the common historical experience, the national identity based on a distinctive culture and the attachment to Hayastan, the homeland of all Armenians.

Contributing to the dynamism of that period was the work of Protestant women missionaries, who established schools, teacher training centers, clinics, and later on orphanages. Through these institutions Armenian women perceived Western trends and attitudes which strengthened their will to reaffirm their Armenian identity and culture with progressive Western ideas.[2]

As education and political awareness gradually eroded the traditional village strictures, Armenian women emerged as the equals of men, with equal responsibilities to achieve the national goals, the first of which was organizing the resistance.

b. National Resistance

Women tried to mobilize the rather passive and demoralized peasantry of Western Armenia by their dedication and self sacrifice for the sake of an Armenian nation free of all

---

[2]Isabel Kaprielian-Churchill, *Polyphony*, The Bulletin of the Multicultural History Society of Ontario, Vol. 4, No. 2, 1982, pp. 5-11.

oppression. "Resist to survive" became the order of the day.

Women organized defense units, secured weapons and ammunition, and hoarded foodstuffs to fight alongside men and survive sieges and blockades. The national struggle inspired perseverance, dedication, and still higher goal setting. During the resistance there was no place for divergence between men's and women's perspectives of their roles. Men and women were equal in the defense of their homeland.

Women had a significant role in mainly the following instances:

a.   Nationalist revolutionary women actually took part in the formation of the Hunchak (1887) and Dashnak (1890) parties and were particularly active in launching the propaganda campaign and the diffusion of forbidden literature aimed at mobilizing the national resistance.

b.   They participated in the early terrorism and self-sacrifice campaign, i.e. occupation of the Ottoman Bank (1896) and the attempt on Sultan Hamid's life (1905).

c.   They participated in the defense of the Baku, Nakhichevan, Yerevan, Zangezur, Karabagh, Gandja, and Tbilisi Armenian communities against Azeri attacks (1905).

d.   They participated in the defense of Sassun (1894, 1915), Zeitun (1895), Van (1908, 1915), Urfa (1915), Shabin-Karahissar (1915), Mussa Ler (1915), and Hajin (1920).[3]

c. Humanitarian Activities and Human Rights Agitation

Women set up a vast network of support services for the mounting numbers of persecution and wartime victims: widows, orphans, refugees, fugitives, wounded or jailed freedom fighters. They also launched economic development

---

[3]For a complete survey of women's participation in the national resistance, see Sona Zeitlian, *Armenian Women in the Revolutionary Movement*, second enlarged edition, Los Angeles, 1992.

projects to provide employment to women to help them become self-sufficient or providers for their families.

Women politicized their staunch defense of basic human rights and propagated a standard of equality and justice for men and women alike. It can be said that nationalist women functioned in a new ideological framework that sustained the rationale for the equal rights movement and allowed them to participate in the process of national liberation. In spite of the patriarchal nature of Armenian society, gender discriminations receded during the national resistance.

Armenia became an independent republic three years after the Genocide. Consequently, on May 28, 1918, Armenia became one of the first nations to grant women the right to vote. Armenia also nominated the first ever woman ambassador (Diana Abkar, ambassador to Japan) and had four women holding parliamentary seats.

Undoubtedly this was a tribute to the degree of national consciousness women had manifested and the confidence that, as equal partners, they would actively participate in the laborious process of nation-building after almost six hundred years of subjugation and fragmentation.

Role of Women During the Communist Rule

After barely two years of independence, there was a Communist takeover. During the seven decades of Communist rule, the promise of egalitarian and just society remained elusive. Despite repeated assurances of women's emancipation, economic difficulties and patriarchal attitudes blended together to limit the progress of women in the public sphere.

Women excelled in education, and record numbers of them worked the "double shift" (employment and housework). Moreover, well over two-thirds of the doctors and more than half of the teachers were women, yet few of them reached decision-making levels.[4]

In general, women's civic role was denied and their nurturing role as wives and mothers was stressed. Once again gender definitions served to justify women's inequality.

However Armenian women had an influence and strength beyond their apparent subordination. In fact the family was the nucleus of nationalist pride, patriotic sentiments, keeping alive the Armenian language and heritage, and resistance to the oppressive communist rule, and of course women were central to the family cohesion. Perhaps it was symbolic of this influence that when the Yerevan statue of Stalin, the largest in the Soviet Union, was pulled down in the 1960s, it was replaced by an impressive figure of Mother Armenia, with her hand on the hilt of her half-drawn sword, ever ready to sacrifice for her nation.

Vital and bold nationalism prevalent in Armenia consolidated the ranks of women as a force in the movement that was changing history. This was reminiscent of the nationalistic mood at the turn of the century which enlisted women in the social upheaval of the nation.

Once again nationalism prompted women to join political organizations or politicized their active defense of human rights. For example, on January 20, 1974, Razmik Zograbian, a member of the underground nationalist National Union party, publicly protested against the repression of Armenians by setting fire to a portrait of Lenin in Yerevan's central square.[5]

In 1978 a new Soviet constitution was being approved for the Transcaucasian republics and an attempt was made to eliminate the clause that provided for the preservation of the

---

[4]Ronald Grigor Suny, *Looking Toward Ararat—Armenia in Modern History*, Indiana University Press, 1993, p. 184.

[5]Arkhiv Samizdat, 3076.

native language of the republics. Immediately there were
massive demonstrations in Tbilisi and Yerevan. Large
numbers of Armenian women marched in protest calling for
the dominance of their national language. Finally the central
government gave up its blatant attempt to expand the role of
Russian in the national republics.

In March 8, 1989, five hundred women demonstrated in
Yerevan to uphold the human rights of the unjustly imprisoned members of the nationalist Karabagh Committee. The
protest movement gained in momentum and gave way to
massive demonstrations in favor of the political prisoners.

In time, as in the past, national consolidation went hand
in hand with modernization, eliminating the traditional
political and religious authorities, uprooting the peasantry,
and making way for an industrial service society so familiar
in advanced Western countries[6]

The vitality of Armenian women benefited from the
increased opportunities of the new society which was more
industrial, more urban, better educated, and more mobile.
Women also shared in the heightened national consciousness
and sense of national interest. However the Communist
power structure was not modernized to pave the way for the
long promised egalitarian and just society. Hence expectations for the improvement of the status of women and their
rights were harnessed by rigid restrictions.

LAYING THE GROUNDWORK FOR EQUALITY AND PARTNERSHIP
BETWEEN MEN AND WOMEN IN A DEMOCRATIC SOCIETY

Armenia regained its independence after the collapse of
the Soviet Union (1991). The new nation bent on achieving

---

[6]Ann Sheehy and Elizabeth Fuller, "Armenia and Armenians
in the USSR: Nationality and Language Aspects of the Census of
1979," *Radio Liberty Research Bulletin XXIV*: 24 (3072), June 13,
1980.

democracy has already ratified the Convention on the Elimination of all Forms of Discrimination Against Women, whereas, for example, the United States is still in the prolonged process of considering ratification.

With the improved perspectives that statehood holds, there comes a renewed challenge: to redefine a woman's role from the development and well-being of her family to her role in the community and her participation in decision-making. The challenge is not only to adapt to the changing world, but also to increase public awareness of women's issues and codify women's rights in the new constitution to enable one and all to know and defend their rights.

As women of a fragmented nation (homeland, interior and exterior diaspora), today we have accepted the challenge and chosen the means to deal with it above and beyond all geographic or partisan considerations. First, to communicate on the basis of mutual respect and trust. Second, to identify the all important issues and goals. Third, to develop concrete plans and strategies to serve as a blueprint for action.

The goal of the women's rights movement is to promote equality and partnership between men and women in our homeland and diasporan communities as well. After seventy years of Communist rule, with an inbuilt mistrust of government, there is an increased need for women to assume their civic responsibilities and play an active role in the public sphere of the Republic of Armenia. As for the diaspora, it is part of the larger Armenian nation, and the goals of all Armenian women are interconnected.

Give Me Your Mothers and I'll Give You a Nation: Diasporan Armenian Women at the Helm

Isabel Kaprielian-Churchill*

The study of Armenian women, least of all Armenian women in the diaspora, has not been blessed with concerted scholarly attention. This presentation begins to redress such a discrepancy. It sets aside the "kitchen and crochet" syndrome in order to counter the stereotype of Armenian women as acquiescing victims or as willing followers in the shadow of their husbands, and focuses, rather, on their leadership role. Because of the paucity of sources, the research was constrained, so I offer only an overview, somewhat like a parachutist floating to earth, pointing out the hills and vales, the rivers and lakes. The late nineteenth to the first half of the twentieth centuries provide the time frame, and the four topics under discussion today—politics, religion, culture, and organizations—provide the major themes.

POLITICS

One of the dominant figures in recent Armenian political history is Maro Vartanian. Born in Tiflis in 1864 in a middle

*Isabel Kaprielian-Churchill is a research associate at the Ontario Institute for Studies in Education at the University of Toronto. Her paper was delivered at the AIWA Annual Meeting in May 1994.

class family, Maro graduated from the Tiflis gymnasium for girls and, against her family's wishes, travelled to St. Petersburg to study physics or medicine at the university —hardly common choices for university-bound women of her period. In the capital city she was drawn into a group of "radical" students and writers embroiled in the cause of liberty and the working class. Pursued by the tsarist secret police, she eventually fled St. Petersburg for Paris. With her fiancé and future husband, Avedis Nazarbekian, she then settled in Geneva, ostensibly to continue her education.

The Nazarbekians and other young Armenian leftist students formed a small band of political activists and intellectuals who discussed the burning questions of the day with leading leftist thinkers. They embraced Marxism and fervently believed that only revolutionary tactics could free Armenians from the stranglehold of their Turkish oppressors. With the zeal and commitment of the young, they drew up the Manifesto of the Armenian Social Democrat Hunchakian party (1887) calling for the liberation of Armenians and the creation of a socialist state. Determined to bring about political and economic change, this small cohort spearheaded the early activities of the Hunchak party in the Ottoman Empire.

Enmeshed in the thick of discourse, Maro was elected to the party executive and to the editorial board of the party organ, *Hunchak* (Bell). But Maro was also a woman of action. During the 1890s she was dispatched to Beirut and Damascus, and eventually to Cilicia, to promote the party and its cause. With characteristic audacity and iron will, she travelled incognito and in disguise from town to town, holding clandestine meetings, raising money, winning converts, and organizing cadres of like-minded insurgents. It goes without saying that Maro was not the only Hunchak working in Cilicia, but she was enough of a threat to the Turkish government that she was imprisoned and an attempt was made on her life.

After her breakup with Nazarbek and following the first Russian Revolution (1905), Maro returned to Tiflis. Throwing herself once again into the political fray, she was, once again, arrested and imprisoned (1910). Her case became a cause célèbre, her impassioned supporters marching with placards and clamoring, "free Maro," "liberate the Armenian Joan of Arc." Russian authorities spared her life but convicted her of anti-tsarist propaganda and sentenced her to hard labor in Siberia. Released after the Russian Revolution in 1917 (she and her daughter spent almost six years in exile), she continued her political activities, this time agitating for a rapprochement between the Hunchakians and the Bolsheviks. In doing so, she contributed to the demise of the social democratic movement in the Caucasus— the movement she herself had helped to found forty years earlier. She died in Tiflis in 1941.

You have only to read Robert Mirak's *Torn Between Two Lands* to understand what a profound and widespread impact the Hunchakian party, its platform, and its internecine warfare had among Armenians in the Ottoman Empire and in the fledgling Armenian communities in North America. As for the beautiful and fiery Maro Vartanian Nazarbekian, regardless of what may be said about her political ideology and strategy, she was as progressive, as committed to her cause, and as brilliant as her contemporary, Rosa Luxembourg. But unlike her fellow radical, Maro Vartanian as a political thinker and writer, as a political activist and organizer, has achieved no prominent place in the historical record.

The same can be said about another woman of politics, Diana Agaberg Apcar, whose life and work took a totally different turn. Apcar left her birthplace, New Julfa, Iran, as a child, and moved with her family to India. Educated in Calcutta, she married Michael Apcarian, heir to a silk business which plied the trade between India and Japan.

Eventually the young couple settled in Yokohama, where Diana earned a well-deserved reputation for her charitable work among the Japanese. Later, with the flow of Armenian refugees to Japan, she took matters into her own hands and established an Armenian village outside Yokohama, where she housed, fed, and educated the survivors at her own expense.

When Armenia won independence in 1918, Diana Apcar was named ambassador to Japan. She was the first foreign woman to be accepted in the Japanese court at such an exalted level and one of the first women in the world to hold the rank of ambassador. Erudite and articulate, Diana Apcar wrote in both Armenian and English about the condition of the Armenian people and the injustices they were suffering:

> By force they [Turks] took possession of the wealth and culture of [an] ancient civilization which they neither preserved nor embellished, but only squandered and desecrated, and buried under ruins. . . The waters of the Euphrates have run red with blood, but not blood from any battlefield but with the blood of an unarmed population murdered by the government that dominated over them . . .
>
> If ten thousand Moslems had been slaughtered by any Christian government, the whole Moslem world would have been convulsed, but when Christians were slaughtered by the hundred thousands by the Turkish government, powerful Christian governments decreed that the horror should be forgotten . . .
>
> The menace of a militant Islam will grow into such formidable proportions as to imperil in the future the peace of the world. It is necessary for the nations to study the map of Asia before they study the map of Europe.[1]

---

[1]*Armenian Herald*, November 1918, pp. 634-36.

Today, seventy-five years later, her prophetic words have a sinister ring to them.

As in the case of Maro Vartanian, it is impossible, at this stage in the research, to gauge the extent of Apcar's impact or influence, except to mention that some years after her death, when an Armenian visited Japan, he was told by a Japanese dignitary that Diana Apcar, the Armenian, had been a role model for Japanese women.

Women like Vartanian and Apcar were pioneers who tried to effect political change. They were outstanding women who operated not only in an Armenian sphere but also in a larger social and political context. As members of a minority ethnic group, they could have limited their vision to the narrow confines of their ethnic world; instead they used their Armenianness as a point of orientation and lived and worked in a much bigger frame of reference.

THE CHURCH

This discussion of the church will deal principally with the Canadian experience but clear parallels can be drawn with the roles of Armenian women in church communities throughout North America.

Armenians have had women martyrs and saints— Hripsimés and Gayanés. Royal and aristocratic women have stood strong in their faith and have, against formidable odds, built churches and monasteries—women like Queen Ashghen and Queen Parantsem, Princess Khosrovitught, and Mariam Bagratuni. But these notable women lived in the distant past and they no longer serve as contemporary role models. How then should we describe the contributions of women in today's church? Some, like a colleague, may take the position that Armenian women's activities at the present time can be summed up in two phrases—sewing gowns, and making coffee and beoreg. Yet my study of the first Armenian church in Canada gives a totally different picture.

The Church of St. Gregory the Illuminator in St. Catharines, Ontario, was consecrated in 1930, just as the Depression was taking its toll. Numbering about 500 people, the small community was composed primarily of working-class families—factory laborers or small business operators. Most of the men worked in a subsidiary plant of General Motors and most of the shops catered to factory personnel. During the Depression most of the men were laid off, and the shops in turn suffered from the downturn. But children still had to be fed and clothed, mortgages to be paid, and the church to be sustained.[2]

Following the murder of Archbishop Tourian in New York in 1933, the community split. Left with only half the church congregation to support it, the church was tottering on precarious ground. But the young refugee women who had come out in the 1920s, not knowing two words in English, who had been sequestered in their homes and in the Armenian community, now took on outside jobs to bring in capital—as farm help, domestics, cooks. Some ran little cottage industries; others took menial jobs in factories—low-paying and exploitative, but jobs all the same. No doubt the same developments occurred in many factory towns in the United States.

By no means am I suggesting that the women alone kept the church alive, but their contributions were absolutely essential to the survival of the church during those dark years. And those contributions have neither been adequately documented nor sufficiently recognized.

Women's efforts went beyond fundraising. As members of the church board of trustees, they helped to administer the

---

[2]Hygus Torosian, "The First Armenian Church in Canada: St. Gregory the Illuminator Armenian Apostolic Church - 1930 - St. Catharines," *St. Gregory Armenian Apostolic Church, Golden Jubilee, 1930-1980, Commemorative Book*, 1980, np.

church. Interestingly, in 1930, not a single woman was on the board. During the 1950s they began playing a formal role in decision-making. In 1992, except for one man, all the trustees were women.

From the beginning, most of the Sunday School teachers were women. As such, they contributed to the religious and Armenian language education of the young. In more recent times and in different places, women have founded and staffed full-day Armenian schools, for example, the Sisters' Academy in the United States (in Philadelphia and Boston) and the Armenian Catholic Sisters' School in Montreal.

In St. Catharines women added to the beauty of the church service, either as organists or as choir members. One need only mention the name of Lucine Zakarian, the soloist at Echmiadzin, to understand the role of women's musical contributions.

While it is true that women sew gowns, it is also true that they are responsible for some of the most beautiful works of art which adorn the church. Had men done this work, it would no doubt have been viewed as art, but as lace and embroidery are considered women's work, they are seen only as crafts and leisure-time activities. Yet some of this work is as intricate, as exquisite, and as lovely as the most treasured painting, the most delicate miniature. Perhaps some day these artifacts will be appreciated, just as, thanks to the work of Lucy Der Manuelian, we now recognize the role of women in spinning and dying wool and in designing and weaving rugs.

More than that, more even than the private and effective influence on husbands, brothers, and sons, some women, like some men, have embodied the true spirit of Christianity and breathed piety into the church. For Armenians, religious commitment and history are so inextricably entwined as to be almost one. In the twentieth century alone, in the post-genocide period, some survivors, feeling abandoned and disinherited, forsook the church and religion altogether, but others, similarly reeling from the shock of their tragic experiences, found solace in their faith, clung to their beliefs, and perhaps strengthened their bonds of devotion. After the Sovietization of Armenia, furthermore, most of the living church was in the diaspora. At one point, it is estimated, three-fourths of all functioning Armenian churches were in the Spiurk. The faithful, the believers— both elite and rank-and-file, both women and men—kept spirituality alive in the church. By their dedication they helped avert the disaster of the secularization of the church in the diaspora. During times of crises and conflict, moreover, such as the period following Tourian's murder (1933) and the division in the church in 1956, spirituality tempered strident hostilities, imbued a measure of gentleness in the congregation, and acted as a bridge between warring factions.

Zivart Torigian (pseudonym) is an example. Devout even as a teenager, Zivart grew up in a strong Dashnak family in St. Catharines. In 1933 after the split, St. Gregory's sided with Echmiadzin and the Dashnak group built its own club. The tension and bitterness between the two camps were such that no one dared cross the battle lines, but Zivart rejected the division. She attended *badarak* (church services), sang in the church choir, and belonged to the club, all at the same time. It was her piety which prompted both factions to accept her. Thus in her own modest way, Zivart became a role model for the young.

CULTURE

We move now to culture, the third workshop topic.

In the Ottoman Empire, Armenians had schools for girls, women's teachers' colleges, women educators, and women's educational associations. Thanks to the research of Barbara Merguerian, we now know that the Armenian women's educational movement was progressive, and that it was strongly influenced by the work of the North American missionaries.

One of the most prominent Armenian women's educational organizations was the Azkanever Hayuyats Ungerutiun (Patriotic Armenian Women's Association), which was founded in Constantinople in 1879. In its first annual report, the Association emphasized its determination to recruit and train women as teachers, to raise the consciousness of Armenian women, and to facilitate the education of Armenian girls throughout the Ottoman Empire, particularly in the provinces.

Marie Beylerian fervently embraced these goals and made it her life's work to improve the education and advance the welfare of Armenian women. Less well-known than her contemporaries, Serpouhi Dusap, Cybile (Zabel Asadour), and Zabel Essayan, Beylerian is, nevertheless, noteworthy because she founded the first Armenian feminist journal. Entitled *Artemis*, this monthly focused on women's role in the family and in literature. In the first issue, published in Cairo in 1902, Marie wrote:

> It has been my dream to establish an independent Armenian women's publication, to provide Armenian women with an organ, to give them a free voice, an unfettered platform. This revue will deal with the aspirations of Armenian women, will try to rectify the injustice to them, to cultivate their intellectual and physical development, and to promote their equality and liberation.

Marie Beylerian was born in Constantinople in 1877, where she was educated and where she started teaching. Early in her career she was drawn into the Armenian liberation movement, reading prohibited Armenian newspapers like *Armenia* and *Hayastan* and participating in clandestine meetings to discuss the liberation struggle. In

1895, not quite 18, she joined the protest at the Sublime Porte, and as a result of her involvement was hounded by the Ottoman police. She fled to Egypt a year later and there married another Armenian revolutionary, Avo Nakashian. Marie continued teaching, still using her maiden name— an emancipatory act even today—and still working towards her goal of a women's publication. Finally in 1902 she began the publication of *Artemis*. After the Young Turk revolution in 1908 and the deposition of Sultan Abdul Hamid, relaxed travel regulations and a somewhat more liberal regime enabled her to return to Turkey, where she took on the principalship of the Hripsimé girl's school in Smyrna. She fell victim to the genocide.

Beylerian's emphasis on equality between women and men is reflected in the choice of name for her revue. Artemis, the Greek name for the Roman goddess Diana and the Armenian Anahid, was the twin sister of Apollo. Unwilling to be outdone by her brother, Artemis became as fine a hunter and marksman as her twin.

Artemis, the monthly, ran scarcely two years, but its impact seems to have been considerable. *Artemis* enjoyed widespread distribution, for in the few extant copies in my possession are letters from the Russian eEpire, the Caucasus, France, Italy, and Germany. Regarded as radical and inflammatory, it was banned in Turkey. Judging from the contributors and choice of selections, including articles, poems, and/or letters by Alice Stone Blackwell, Tekeyan, Demirjibashian, Kalemkarian, as well as translations of works by such writers as Shelley, Rossetti, and Tolstoy, an attempt was made to bring together various ideas about the role and development of women from a number of countries.

A passionate exchange, for instance, compares the European feminist movement with Armenian feminists. One of the most fascinating aspects of this discourse is the assertion that feminist movements cannot all be the same but must be adapted to the conditions of their national contexts. Another discussion compares the education of women and girls in Europe and the United States with the schooling of Armenian girls. *Artemis* repeatedly appeals to Armenian women of privilege to help in the education of women and children in the lower classes, in both urban and rural environments, and reveals how urban, westernized, middle-class Armenian women tried to assist and uplift their sisters in rural/provincial society.

Beylerian hoped to change attitudes about the place and education of girls. In her writings and in her classes, she promoted equal education for Armenian boys and girls and predicted that educating women would pay phenomenal dividends in the enlightenment of the Armenian people. Marie frequently quoted an old adage which said, "Give me your mothers and I will give you a nation." She offered her own response, "I want to be able to write: 'Here are the mothers; now give us a nation.'"

ORGANIZATIONS

Moving now to the fourth topic, women's organizations, let me focus, once again, on the Canadian experience. In the first half of the twentieth century, two types of women's groups existed in Canada: totally independent ones and those linked to political parties.

Unaffiliated associations were rare, but one was started in Montreal in 1930. At that time scarcely two hundred Armenians had settled in this French-and-English-speaking city. Most of the women were survivors and many had immigrated as picture brides in the 1920s, destined for the pre-1914 settlers. Typically the women came from different geographic origins and different classes and brought with them a host of refugee experiences. They shared two common characteristics—their gender and their ethnic loyalty. As they became acquainted with each other and acclimatized to their new environment, they decided to establish their own autonomous women's group in order to retain their culture and to pass on their heritage to their children. Their Montreal Armenian Women's Cultural Association organized concerts, plays, picnics, and genocide commemoration services. Doubtless their most important contribution was the operation of an Armenian supplementary school, which the women ran for fifteen years. Their voluntarism and diligence enabled a generation of Armenian children to learn to read and write Armenian.

Settlers coming from the Middle East in the late 1950s and 1960s built on the foundations which the women had so painstakingly established. Today Montreal is the largest Armenian settlement in Canada, numbering more than 20,000, with three full-day schools, Saturday schools, summer schools, and Sunday schools. It is estimated that over 60 percent of Armenian children in Montreal of elementary and secondary school age attend some form of Armenian school.

Of the second type of women's organization—the politically oriented ones—the most widespread and enduring one was the Armenian Relief Society. In comparing the ARS in the 1920s, 30s, and 40s with women's organizations of other ethnic groups in Canada during that time, my cursory research reveals that the ARS is outstanding for its role in rendering effective service to the Armenian community and in prompting the development of women.

In Canada the ARS allowed women to serve the community through charitable work, cultural endeavors, and the establishment and maintenance of Armenian language supplementary schools. While it is true that many members were engaged in fundraising work—cooking meals, serving at banquets, selling raffle tickets, preparing handmade fancywork for sale—it is also true that through their enterprises the women created a forum for enhancing both their administrative and Armenian-language skills. Through their meetings and activities the members learned parliamentary procedure and discipline; they learned how to write and respond to minutes, correspondence, and reports, and they learned to speak publicly on topics other than home and family.

Armenian women's organizations gave the young refugees opportunities to develop themselves in a new and unfamiliar world. This especially applied to educated and/or bright women who could fulfill intellectual and artistic needs and still remain within the perimeters of the Armenian community, safe from the corruption of Canadian society —the "painted" *odars* with loose morals.

In their pursuit of ethnocultural goals, women's organizations invariably became vital channels in broadening the scope and nurturing the talents of Armenian women. Almost one hundred years ago Marie Beylerian advocated educating mothers for the resurgence of the nation. Women's organizations, though outside the formal milieu of schools, combined commitment to the cultural development of the ethnic group with individual development and emerged as critical vehicles for enlightening mothers, educating children, and strengthening the identity of the Armenian community in the diaspora.

Today, as Armenians stand on the threshold of the next century, as new political realities confront them, as the young Republic struggles to survive against almost insurmountable odds, groups of women are joining together, like AIWA, to succor Armenia, and in doing so are not only revitalizing and rekindling an Armenian spirit in the diaspora, but are winning the support of young Armenians who might otherwise reject their ancestral heritage and identity.

CONCLUSION

As I pondered about outstanding women of the past and about committed women in the present, I had to ask myself if there was something binding these disparate souls together. I wondered whether they were a cacophony of voices, out of tune with each other, or whether there was some harmony. Gradually, I began to see them as a jazz band, each one playing her own instrument, improvising in her own way, but all bound together by a single melody. It was, however, easier to find such an analogy than to find a specific word in either English or Armenian to describe that melody. The words "nationalism" or "*askasirutiun*" are clearly inappropriate.

After much tossing about, for want of a better word, I finally settled on ethno-patriotism. Ethno-patriotism describes the loyalty which members of the Spiurk feel for their homeland. Ethno-patriotism defines a commitment to a land in which diasporan Armenians have never lived and some have never even visited. Ethno-patriotism represents allegiance to a culture and hope for its people.

Speech Over Silence: The Pen and the Needle in Armenian Women's Auto-biographies

Gayane Karen Merguerian[*]

In the past twenty years a number of autobiographical writings by Armenian women, particularly women who have survived the genocide, have begun to appear in the English-language press. In many cases the writings have appeared at the urging of relatives and friends of the author. They include valuable eyewitness accounts of Turkish atrocities, and their descriptions of daily life have made an important contribution to the fragmented written history of Armenian communities before 1915.

Beyond "bearing witness" to life in the old country and the years of genocide and upheaval, however, these auto-biographies also deserve to be examined for their contributions to the history and literature of women in the diaspora. This paper focuses specifically on the strategies which the authors employ in order to articulate their identities, both as Armenians and as women. I shall argue that when they examine their lives, they find themselves rejecting cultural ideologies of gender and cultural expectations for the patterns of women's lives.

*Gayane Karen Merguerian is Government Documents Librarian and Social Sciences Coordinator at the Seton Hall University Library in South Orange, New Jersey.

What do I mean by cultural ideologies of gender? For women of both Armenian and non-Armenian descent, autobiography-writing has special meaning, because it implies an assertion of the power of self-definition in a culture which perpetually seeks to define woman, and to define her as the "other." Feminist critics beginning with Simone de Beauvoir have noted that the world of letters is a traditionally male world, one in which women are described and written about, but one in which their own literary production is ignored and devalued. In the Armenian village in Turkey even women's oral speech used to be circumscribed. For example, a young daughter-in-law was not supposed to speak to her mother-in-law until she bore her first son. Photographs and anthropological research have shown that young married women wore a black kerchief across their mouths until the speech-making power identified with the presence of the son allowed them to lift it. Women in the Armenian community, especially at the beginning of this century, were not supposed to tell their own stories, or attempt to give meaning to their own lives. They were supposed to be written *about* by the "real" literary giants of the autobiographical genre, such as Vahan Totoventz.

Even among the second generation in the United States, the literature of Armenian identity formation (which is a kind of autobiography) is dominated by the figure of Michael Arlen, whose *Passage to Ararat* is considered a classic although no women, including his wife who figures prominently in the book, are named in it. If woman is the object in this literature, then by putting pen to paper and writing her own life she challenges silence, the culturally imposed ideology of the female gender. I would argue that this insistence on the right to speak for herself is at once a feminist and a political act. Both within and outside the Armenian community, the woman autobiographer removes the black kerchief.

We, as feminist readers, may celebrate the affirmation of courage implied by the autobiographical act, but it is also important to remember that, for many genocide survivors, the thought of writing unleashes feelings not of affirmation or liberation but of desperation, anger, and pain. Many of them devote long passages to the subject of writing and what writing means to them. Ramela Martin, for example, survived the genocide and escaped to the United States only to be diagnosed with tuberculosis soon after her arrival. Finding herself orphaned, shut off from the world in a sanatorium, and feeling excluded on account of her sex from the world of letters, she fantasizes about writing. But because she doesn't know whether she will survive physically, or whether she is capable of writing her way to survival, her dreams are awash in the blood of a threefold death: first, death by the spilling of blood in genocide; second, death by a disease—tuberculosis —characterized by coughing up blood; and third, death by the silence imposed on her sex. (After all, her models in the following passage are men, and the blood of death and disease may also be the blood of menstruation):

> At times I was a writer, a woman Thomas Wolfe or a female Dostoyevsky, turning myself inside out for all the world to see, letting my guts gush forth, revealing everything, dredging up every detail, emptying myself as a bucket of blood upon the earth, hoping to stain it for all eternity.[1]

For Martin, to write her autobiography later in life is to do more than speak out as a woman, or to interrogate prevailing ideologies of gender. It is literally to inscribe herself into presence in a world which would otherwise have recorded

---

[1]Ramela Martin, *Out of Darkness* (Cambridge, Mass.: Zoryan Institute, 1989), p. 177.

nothing but her absence.

For Armenian women autobiographers, then, writing means more than the articulation of identity, it means survival, and it means survival on two levels: as Armenian and as woman. But this leads to particular problems. On the one hand, the authors hope, and their audience generally expects, that their writing will contribute to the preservation of the historical record of their community, that they will celebrate Armenian identity and ensure its survival. On the other hand, as women looking for survival through writing, they criticize and undermine the patriarchal foundations of that same community and identity. How do these authors attempt to open up a critical space in which to negotiate the conflicting demands of gender identity on the one hand and ethnic identity on the other? A useful point of departure for examining possible answers to this question is that potent symbol of Armenian female identity, the needle.

For Armenian women the needle is generally associated with the art of making lace, for which they used to be, and in some places still are, well-known. A few women note with pride in their autobiographies that their mothers knew how to sew and make lace, and they regret not having learned how to do it themselves. Among women who were actually required to learn it, however, taking up the needle symbolized putting aside child's play, and beginning to locate identity in gender differentiation and in (hetero) sexuality. In both village and town the needle was the instrument by which the marriage dowry was traditionally prepared—hence the link between being a girl and making lace, between female sexuality and a culturally imposed female gender identity.

In the orphanages, lace was made for sale. Hannah Kalajian says she learned to make lace in an orphanage in Constantinople by watching older girls and picking up discarded scraps of thread to practice on. She was vaguely aware that lace-making was associated with being "older" for some reason, but for her, still prepubescent and sexually inexperienced, it was not something in which she located, or was required to locate, her sexual identity. She remembers feeling "a small satisfaction" at her successes.[2] Others deliberately tried to learn lacemaking out of appreciation and respect for the tradition. "My stay in Aintab was too short to master the different stages of this complicated art, which took years to master," Tamam Zarouhi Getsoyan laments.[3]

Getsoyan and Kalajian, then, did not see the occupation of lacemaking as burdensome. But then, their first experiences were strictly optional. A far more common reaction among the many Armenian women who had to learn to sew or make lace was anger, rebellion, even hatred. For Shipley, the relationship between the needle and the gender role she was expected to perform was explicit. Sewing separated her physically as well as symbolically from her male playmates, a fact which she deeply resented:

> Brokenhearted, I watched the boys through the window. Without saying a word, Mother led me away, put a sock in my hands, and asked me to mend it. . . To be a lady from that day on, when the boys gathered to play stick-ball, Mother sent me to a very strict woman with five and seven-year old children to teach me proper Armenian etiquette, the art of Armenian lace, and other handwork.[4]

This relationship between sewing and the forcible

---

[2]Hannah Kalajian, *Hannah's Story* (Belmont, Mass.: Armenian Heritage Press, 1990), p. 22.

[3]Naomi Topalian, *Dust to Destiny* (Watertown, Mass.: Baikar, 1986), p. 13.

[4]Alice Muggerditchian Shipley, *We Walked, Then Ran* (Meza, Az.: Print Peddler, 1983), p. 35.

imposition of gender identity is reinforced in a succeeding passage in the book, a passage eerily reminiscent of the legends of Sleeping Beauty and Snow White, in which the entrance into the female sexual domain is signified by the pricking of a woman's finger on a forbidden spindle. Shipley joins with the princesses of fairy-tale lore, spilling the symbolic blood of menarche, except that unlike the fairy tale princesses, she does not prick *herself*:

> She taught me the graceful way of sitting on a cushion and the dainty way of holding the needle between thumb and forefinger with the thimble on the mid-finger and my little finger curled up delicately above my ring finger. She watched me like a hawk. Any abrogation of her instructions brought the sharp prick of a long darning needle on my knuckles, making them bleed.[5]

The needle became for Shipley an instrument of punishment, in her memory, gender as a social construct (you are a girl, therefore you must sew) was associated with pain and blood via the needle.

For other autobiographers, the needle was seen as the undesirable antithesis of a similarly shaped object, the pen. For despite the undisputed artistic value of Armenian lace, the women who wrote their autobiographies saw immediately and clearly that the act of writing was a far more powerful tool of self-expression than sewing or lacemaking. Indeed, the contrast between needle, representing traditional female roles, and pen, representing the male world of letters, is made in the Anglo-American literary tradition as well. The American poet Anne Bradstreet said, "I am obnoxious to each carping tongue/ Who says my hand a needle better fits," and Margaret Cavendish said that she was "addicted . . . to write

---

[5]Ibid., p. 36.

with the pen [rather] than to work with the needle."[6]

In the case of Serpoohie Christine Jafferian, the comparison is just as explicit. Like Shipley, Jafferian resists the traditional gender role that her mother and other women impose on young girls through teaching them to sew. However Jafferian also sees in the needle the denial of her dream to write. Her feelings on the subject are so strong she attempts to sabotage the sewing project which she and her mother are working on together:

> I just didn't like to sew . . . I had no intention of becoming a dressmaker. My dreams were about America. When I grew older, somehow I would get there, go to school, *become a famous writer*, acquire plenty of money, and have an abundant amount of clothes made especially for me. . . Mother turned away for a second. Grasping the opportunity, I made an angry movement with the scissors in my hands. To my horror, a one inch cut was made down the V-neckline. Mother found a way of fixing it. My dreams forgotten for the time being, I submitted to her will and made the dress.[7] (Italics mine)

Like Jafferian, Dirouhi Kouymjian Highgas confronts her grandmother's insistence on the incompatibility of the female role and the world of letters when her grandmother insists that she not attend high school:

> She [my grandmother] must have noticed the expression of disappointment on my face. "It is very hard to get

---

[6]Mary C. Mason, "The Other Voice: Autobiographies of Women Writers," *Autobiography: Essays Theoretical and Critical*, James Olney, ed. (Princeton, NJ: Princeton University Press, 1980), p. 212-13.

[7]Serpoohie Christine Jafferian, *Winds of Destiny* (Belmont, Mass.: Armenian Heritage Press, 1993), pp. 81-82.

married if you have too much education," she explained.
"No man wants a wife with her nose stuck in a book all
day long. We will send you to dressmaking school . . ."[8]

Even when they tried to use the needle for practical
purposes, to empower themselves financially, it ultimately let
these women down:

> I remember getting a job in a training program of some
> sort. Mainly we sit all day monogramming initials on
> napkins, tablecloths, towels, or sometimes handkerchiefs.
> Not much of a challenge to someone who learned to
> make intricate Armenian lace in the orphanage in
> Constantinople . . . I don't think my destiny lies in a
> never-ending pile of linens.[9]

In contrast, winning a fountain pen as a school prize after
months of hard work and determined study transports
Kalajian into a reverie about her future and the promise it
holds:

> I sit at the table, pen in hand. Its graceful tapered point
> shines in the moonlight coming in the window, and for a
> while I am hypnotized. But then my mind looks inward,
> at myself. In these few months I have become my own
> person. I feel something in me, a kind of power. What is
> it? . . . I guess it's a kind of faith that there are answers
> to any problems, and I will look for answers. I go to bed
> feeling, for the first time in my life, a joy in being alive,
> and in knowing who I am.[10]

---

[8]Dirouhi Kouymjian Highgas, *Refugee Girl* (Watertown, Mass.:
Baikar Press, 1985), p. 111.

[9]Kalajian, *Hannah's Story*, p. 51.

[10]Ibid., p. 34.

Kalajian's feeling about the power of the pen and its relationship to her identity echoes that of a very different woman, an Armenian-Russian daughter of wealthy parents and someone who had access to a solid and extensive formal education: the poet Nina Berberova. Berberova's description of how she felt when she wrote her first poem as a child is startlingly similar to Kalajian's passage above, despite their differences in class and experience. They both felt the impulse to written self-representation as a life impulse; as women they cherished it, and refused to take it for granted:

> On those evenings when snow fell, the windows froze, and I was overcome with expectations in that atmosphere, the initial music of genuine life, eagerness to live and know one's self, which forced me to shudder at its seriousness and grandeur as it resounded in me through those childish verses. I remember that feeling with my entire body. When I experienced them, and that is now most precious to me, the solemnity, responsibility, and uniqueness of those moments were clear to me. It seemed I heard, in jolts, my own sprouting into the future.[11]

Looking back at their lives, women do sometimes admit the practical advantages of knowing how to sew. Nevertheless, there is no romanticization of the needle arts among the older generation. In fact, both Kalajian and Highgas attempt to give the needle new life and power, but in both cases the attempts fail. Highgas covered gold coins with cloth and then sewed them like covered buttons in long rows on her dresses, in an attempt to smuggle her savings out of Turkey. But the weight of the clothing attracted the attention of Turkish

---

[11]Nina Berberova, *The Italics Are Mine* (New York: Chatto & Windus, 1991), p. 43.

guards, who tore it apart and confiscated the coins. The female/Armenian needle was powerless against the forces of male/Turkish aggression. Kalajian's mother sewed money into her dress for the transatlantic journey to the United States. But when a kindly American aboard the ship gave Kalajian a brand new dress, Kalajian "accidentally" threw the old one overboard (though the action may in fact have been deliberate), forgetting about the money which was sewn into its seams. The dress her mother made and the currency, both figurative and literal, which her mother stitched into it were discarded when she entered the new world.

By comparing the needle unfavorably with the pen, and using sewing as a symbol of the weakness and vulnerability of women's lives in the old country, these autobiographers question culturally defined gender and ethnic roles. They recognize the fact that while they were preparing their dowries, men were being trained to join the world of learning and letters, a world where the true promise of public self-expression and assertion of identity reside.

And yet it comes as no surprise that the second generation of the diaspora, whose mothers and grandmothers worked so hard to liberate themselves from the needle, had occasion to regret not learning how to sew. After all, it does have its uses, as Arlene Avakian, who grew up in an environment of conservative wealth and privilege in the United States, testified. In the following passage she and her friends try in vain to keep up with the latest fashions:

Rachel and I had to find ways to supplement the less than adequate wardrobes our mothers agreed to buy for us. We tried to sew, but our efforts yielded only barely presentable skirts sorely in need of belts to cover botched waistbands. Blouses and dresses were beyond our skill.[12]

Recently feminist historians and social scientists like Mary Daly and others have gone beyond Avakian's mild regret and undertaken an affirmative reevaluation of the needle arts of their female forebears; this approach is reflected in a remarkable poem by Diana Der Hovanessian, a second-generation Armenian American whose work is highly autobiographical. In "Armenian Needlework" Der Hovanessian attempts to reclaim lace as both an art form and a political act.

Armenian Needlework

I.

Here is the snowflake that never melts.
Here is the map of a past, replaced.

Here, where Arachne's needle flew
into Asdghik's clouds, piercing through

old patterns, edging the dream
woven by peasant, princess and queen.

Here are old fables, elaborate, fine,
prophecy, fantasy, patience entwined.

Here is the snowflake that never melts,
and time itself preserved in Armenian lace.

II.

We have always miniaturized.
Look at our paintings, small, precise.

---

[12]Arlene Voski Avakian, *Lion Woman's Legacy: An Armenian-American Memoir* (New York: Feminist Press, 1992), p. 35.

We have always minimized.
Look at our story, pressed into lies.

Look at our country, boundary capsized.
swords shrunk to needles, daintily sized,

ready to make lace or put out eyes.[13]

The first stanzas of the poem establish the needle as a female tool, but not a mundane nor even an oppressive one; in fact it is used by princesses and queens. The lace is like the quiet snowflake, except that it "never melts"; it is a permanent record of Armenian history and identity. But in the second set of stanzas Der Hovanessian recognizes lace's limitations; it is "miniaturized" like the "small, precise" paintings of the illuminated Gospels. Furthermore, like "our story, pressed into lies" it may be deformed, along with the country, its modern-day boundaries "capsized." Then, in the second-to-last line, Der Hovanessian suddenly calls for a new use for the needle, not as a pen but as a sword, in the service of warfare rather than history. Suddenly it is not only ready to make lace, but to commit an act of violence, to "put out eyes." In the first stanza of the poem, Der Hovanessian has transformed the needle from the symbol of a passive and circumscribed female role, the antithesis of written self-expression, to the tool of Arachne and the cartographers, perhaps even a possible substitute for the pen. But in the second stanza she questions its value as a lacemaking tool, however precious the lace, preferring to "elevate" it to the status of an unabashed weapon of aggression, albeit one which, she regrets, is only "daintily sized."

For those autobiographers who were required to sew and make lace, writing about sewing became a way to defy the

---

[13]Diana Der Hovanessian, *Songs of Bread, Songs of Salt* (New York: Ashod Press, 1990), p. 49.

silence and anonymity the needle imposed on their mothers and grandmothers, and would have imposed on them as well. It is important, then, for us to resist likening the needle either to the pen or to the sword, if by doing so we detract from the reality of its tyranny over so many Armenian women. In fact, the very existence of Der Hovanessian's published poems, whatever she says about lacemaking, is testimony to her awareness that it is writing rather than sewing which gives us the power to inscribe identity on our own terms, to create maps, to never melt, to survive. The Armenian women discussed in this paper defied society's expectations of gender and ethnicity when they overthrew the stifling powerlessness of needlework in favor of the pen. They had it right. Our interpretive strategies should celebrate their triumph, a triumph of speech over silence.

The Role of Armenian Women in the Preservation of Armenian Identity in France: Some Social Aspects of the Transmission of a Communal Memory

Martine Hovanessian[*]

WOMEN AND THE DEFENSE OF "ARMENIANNESS" (*L'ARMÉNITÉ*)
A study of the Armenian community during the course of four generations settled since the years 1922-1923[1] in the region of Paris provides evidence of attempts at integration into the normative orientation of the welcoming or adoptive society—attempts which were accompanied nonetheless by forms of allegiance to a communal bond.

This bond was realized by putting into place at a very early stage cultural, religious, and political organizations providing the maintenance of *hayabahbanum*, that is to say the preservation of "Armenianness" (*"l'Arménité"*). These organizations, despite their limited means, have nonetheless encouraged the regular meeting of families and the delineation of spaces of the *entre-soi* (interrelatedness), inscribed henceforth on the communal landscape. In addition these

---

[*]*Martine Hovanessian is a researcher at the National Center for Scientific Research in Strasbourg, France, in the Department of Society, Law, and Religion in Europe.*

[1]Martine Hovanessian, *Le lien communautaire—Trois générations d'Arméniens* (Paris: Editions Armand Colin, 1992).

units of association, modest for the most part, have permitted in their wake the formulation of collective projects and their reinterpretation by succeeding generations on those urban territories.[2]

The genesis of these organizations provides clear evidence of the active participation of women, notably in the teaching of the Armenian language to children and in activities for the social benefit of the most deprived refugees and the elderly, as well as their active mobilization for the building of places of worship and the advancement of the Armenian press in France.

The social history of the Armenian community indicates that, in the heart of communal organizations, some of them will bring forth leaders in the Armenian cause and will engage in community debates to defend the national claims of a minority dispersed and tested by history. Most of these women are sympathetic to the Dashnak party, which preserves in the dispersion the inalienable sense of ancestral lands and the theme of the reunification of the territories.

Certainly militant women directly involved in political pronouncement are rare; the presence of women is more notable in their devotion to the community, where they hold a rather limited power of decision. However, memory preserves some names of women celebrated for their declared "patriotism," and this phenomenon reveals a women's movement, still weak, toward equality and away from their traditional condition of guardian of the hearth. These women have been apparently sensitized to new ideas of democratization which were registered prior to the 1915 genocide, in a historical process of secularization of the national consciousness. One can well see the weight of this phenomenon in the

---

[2]Martine Hovanessian, *Les Arméniens et leurs territoires* (Paris: Editions Autrement, 1995).

writer Zabel Essayan, militant in the national cause, in her autobiographical novel about her childhood in Constantinople at the turn of the century.[3] The author rebels against a conservatism/traditionalism conveyed at the same time by the church and by the values of a very rigid family hierarchy.

The representatives of political authority remain, however, the men, while their women busy themselves in auxiliary activities, most of which are leisure activities, educational projects, and above all works of Armenian benevolence. The women thus contribute to maintain at all cost the political ideologies by transforming them into social settings, by distilling them in satellite associations (choral, scout, weekly school, dance class) whose principal objective consists of keeping together the young generations, some of whom will become militants in the Armenian cause and will be active in the political parties.

In whatever way, women are invested with an educational power flowing largely from the framework of their own family unit, in order "to perpetuate the life of the nation," a recurrent theme in the Armenian press of the diaspora and the chronicles of community life.

But the role of transmission assumed by the Armenian woman in France cannot be understood uniquely by her participation in the structure of the social space which will continually evolve; thus during a dozen years one finds her in the lay committees of the Apostolic church or as the responsible figure in socio-political organizations.

The stories of the life and the family histories of generations of Armenians in France stress essentially the values which the women have conveyed through their role of recasting family cohesion, a cohesion remaining very depen-

---

[3]Zabel Essayan, *Les Jardins de Silidhar* (Paris: Albin Michel, 1994).

dent, in conditions of exile, on the demands of work and on the overseeing of the economic universe.

We cannot comprehend the social interests and the hopes of the Armenians of the exodus, which are constituted around the universe of the family, without taking into account the very nature of the rupture with the society of origin which has fractured the processes of identification[4] and has transformed women in some way into heroines of family and national legend,[5] taking away from them at the same time any aspect of individual choice.

THE ROLES OF KINSHIP IN THE TRADITIONAL ARMENIAN FAMILY

Emile Benvéniste, in the "vocabulary of Indo-European institutions," reconstructs beginning with the vocabulary of kinship the family structure which takes form through this vocabulary: *that of a patriarchal society resting on a paternal line of descent (filiation) and realizing the model of a large family with an ancestor around whom are grouped all the male descendants and their family units.*

Until the end of the nineteenth century, this type of large patrilineal and patrilocal family prevailed in the countryside. In the second half of the nineteenth century families consisted of forty or fifty, or even sixty to seventy persons.

Remarkable by the solidarity of its bonds, the family was

---

[4]Let us emphasize the fact that the family unit among the Armenians, referring to a true social organization, was dismantled by the catastrophe of 1915. There resulted in this regard a disequilibrium of the sexes, to the profit of the female sex, since the men, *holders of the line of descent*, were eliminated by priority.

[5]In the Armenian language, the terms "family" and "nation" are derived from the same root.

distinguished by the codification of relations between men and women, between the generations, by a moral system permeated with religious values (courage, fidelity, honor), and by an economic organization in which the "great house" was sufficient in itself to supply all needs.

"The last fortress to protect,"[6] the family was invested as a substitute for a sovereign state, with great responsibilities in power formation, in the very strict moral code, and in economic life. J.-P. Mahé[7] demonstrates how, in the contemporary Armenian language, the hierarchy even of terms relating to kinship reveals a canonical model of family organization. Extremely rich and codified, this vocabulary distinguishes interior kinship and the consanguine—that is to say the women pledged to remove themselves from the grand house because of marriage: the sister does not belong to the interior kinship; she is officially detached from the clan of the father and incorporated into the clan of the father-in-law. Besides, as to the issue of an analysis of the dissymmetry of the terms of kinship, the author concludes that these relate to the man. It in effect perpetuates the name of the clan.

This power of transmission confers upon the man a true social authority, which requires, of course, that he fulfill a certain number of duties and obligations and disengages him from the kinship by marriage. The husband in effect is not required to maintain day-to-day relations with the members of his in-law family; his only interlocutor is the representative of the allied family: the father of his wife.

---

[6]See Claire Mouradian and Anahide Ter Minassian, "Permanence de la famille arménienne," *Cultures et sociétés de l'Est* (Paris, No. 9, 1988), 59-84.

[7]Jean-Pierre Mahé, "Structures sociales et vocubulaire de la parenté en arménien contemporain," *Revue des études arméniennes* (xviii), 1985.

The wife in return, the future spouse, must submit to an ensemble of strict customs, leaving her little occasion to manage her personal time or even less to exercise her free will. Even more, she is constrained to be mute and must respond by signs to the tyrannical commands of her mother-in-law. The latter in effect directs the work of the household. In fact, the only power of the woman corresponds with her age and resides in the transmission of her knowledge of the administration of the domestic work. Submissive to the law of her husband, whom she never addresses by his first name but as "*Mart*" ("Man") according to custom, she is compelled to respect a certain number of institutionalized rules at the heart of her in-law family.

This conservative family structure is the typical model of the collective bond. It provides resistance to exogenous influences. However it does not exist in matrimonial alliances between ethnic groups. If the marriage, most often arranged by the elder of the clan, must conform to a fundamental rule (a ban on alliance between close and distant cousins), it must however be negotiated within the larger community.

SOCIAL ROLES OF WOMEN IN THE PRESERVATION OF THE ARMENIAN IDENTITY IN FRANCE

It is necessary to understand how an ancient model, which for centuries fashioned, along with the language and the religion, a sense of belonging to "the nation," constituted one of the organizational principles of the community in France, although this model was to undergo numerous recompositions in conditions of exile.

Through this process, what precisely has been the role of women? Which social usages of kinship have they made to reconstitute the unity of the family cell and to guarantee for it a new dominion?

No doubt the integration of Armenians in France necessitated the active participation of women in the economic planning of the home. This participation was not without effect in changing cultural and marital behavior. Thus it was for endogamous marriage, which was to become less and less frequent after 1946; likewise the Armenian family, which had been rather prolific, during the years 1950 to 1960 with the second generation was to become a family with two or three children. Besides, the fact that the women were led, beginning with the first generation, against the dictates of tradition, to leave the home for rough factory work led progressively to the relaxation of the cultural codes. Thus, beginning with the second generation, the preference turned away from prearranged marriage, which in turn diminished the number of marriages arranged between families without the consent of the future spouses. The rigid codification of intra-family relations such as described above underwent transformations all the more radical as to forced exile were added new modes of urban life, different stages of migration, and the cultural shock produced by contact with industrial societies in which the concepts of the family were very different.

THE "ENTRE-SOI"

The consequences of the removal of the Armenians from their territories[8] led in France to the elaboration of a double process: on the one hand the Armenians were animated by a wish to reinvent the "village" with the end of assuring again to the family its territorial seat. Thus in the urban milieu one observes the formation of distinct Armenian quarters which respect scrupulously the regional differences in effect in the

---

[8]Let us recall that the majority of those exiled during the years 1923 to 1930 to France were of rural origin. A study of the geographical origin of Armenians living in the region of Paris, Rhone-Alps, and Bouches-du-Rhone indicates that ten percent only were originally from seaports or from large cities.

Ottoman Empire. On the other hand, these practices of appropriating space favoring village solidarities permitted the regroupment of homes and the consolidation of family unity.

As a consequence, these attempts at settlement were to evolve toward the elaboration of an image of continuity; the Armenians in effect would claim back progressively a communal status in the territories of their inscription.

The women came to be at the heart of these communal stakes, to the extent that they participated very concretely in the emancipation of the Armenian from the stigmatism of the worker-immigrant, a movement which works both to rehabilitate an ethno-cultural identity and to restore a memory.

The women of the first generation (those of the exodus), then of the second, were to be from adolescence asked to sustain this collective willingness combining two imperatives: to have the family acquire a validating social status and "to reclaim a lost dignity." Thus they were to mix with their very strict duties as mother and spouse a project of economic survival. The accumulation of these roles constitutes one of the first constraints of immigration and marks a rupture with the society of origin. But it does not witness in reality a process of acculturation; on the contrary, if the Armenian woman in exile has to "earn money," this new economy of the family in the long run bears a communal perspective: to recreate the conditions of cultural autonomy; to recreate the hierarchical cadres and the symbols of a collective. Her earnings as couturier at home or as a worker favors the purchase of a house, which permits in turn the gradual resumption of artisan activity in the private spheres (small commerce, mail-order business). Often confined to the home with many tasks to be conducted, reconciling the duties of housewife and economic provider, watching the children, working to finish up sewing in order to meet an urgent order of a patron, an older person sometimes to care for, the women of the two first generations have, contrary to custom, multiple roles. They become, despite themselves, the pivot of the social interaction of the family and permit the husband access to professional independence.

Women's contributions in the process of accumulating money, or acquiring capital, very intense in the post-war years, created subsequently in the 1960s in the region of Paris a category of entrepreneurial women in knitting or in confectionery. A strong collaboration between the two first generations was to initiate them into the trade of couture, or in the weaving and mounting of patterns; evidence is provided by the transformation of part of the apartment into a workshop in which they acquire the psychological advantages of independent workers. The woman, "while earning her living," thus maintained despite the ruptures occasioned by immigration one of the aspects of the social norm: to remain in the private sphere and to supervise the education of the children.[9]

One clearly sees here how the economic plan underlies the transmission of values conveyed by the family in which the members undertake to preserve the connection of proximity and of dependence. The sharing in the same activity in the heart of the family offers a reassuring framework of adaptation, not imposed by an exterior constraint, and permits the remaining aloof from certain norms conveyed by French society. These trades will assist in the pursuit of a socio-cultural logic in which work and social life, professional activity and private life, do not form two separate

---

[9]One observes in our time in the Parisian region this same phenomenon among the newcomers originally from Turkey. Many of them choose to work at home: the industry of knitting in full growth in the community of Issy-les-Moulineaux, and which developed thanks to the Armenians permits these Armenian women to watch their young children, whom they do not entrust to collective settings such as nurseries.

spheres, but one and the same unity.

The women of the second generation favor the possibility for the husband to find "true" work outside. They permit men who in France are not absolutely identified with a working culture to quit harsh labor in the factory in order to pursue certain professions carried out in the country. Thus they have provided the means to renew a culture of trades in which priority is accorded to professional independence.

From the first generation to the second, we witness an enlargement of the professional range; the commerce of artisans carried on by Armenians develops after the war. The possession of a small personal business, as well as the construction of a home, provides the fundamental unities for the preservation of a belonging. If the house protects the family and permits it to withdraw from others, the economic space on the other hand facilitates Armenian sociability and the maintenance of communal habits.

WOMEN CAUGHT BETWEEN THE DESIRE FOR EMANCIPATION AND DUTY

Women have thus maintained the phenomenon of withdrawing within themselves, which for two generations permitted the family to be reconstituted. But this spirit of devotion, imposed by social constraints and reinforced by moral values induced by an ethno-religious tradition, has truly been detrimental to their personal emancipation. Submissive still in the second generation to the laws of a patriarchal society (limitation of their exit to the exterior, control by the father or in his absence by the brother), they are directly touched by these bonds of captivity to the past, exacerbated by the fact that Armenians perceive their condition of uprooting as definitive and therefore seem crushed under the obsession to conserve a patrimony in the larger sense.

Much testimony collected concerning women of the first

and the second generations retraces their obsession to work and their renunciation of all ambition for personal fulfillment. The priority has been to guarantee the transmission of a patrimony of goods and of values to future generations in order to provide them with the possibility of reaching a better social status and thus to avoid identification with a history of destitution, a history that overwhelms the senses.

Many women could not take advantage of the opening offered by the new welcoming society; thus they often gave up tertiary trades (that of typist, for example) more open to relations with the public, in order to rejoin the family enterprise.

Witnesses to the servility and social humiliation of the first generations, they relate to a universe of psychological constraints, and their repressed desire to "leave" the family milieu or the Armenian quarter appears in their testimony as having been radically opposed to the concepts of the first generation, in which the sense of family supersedes individual happiness.

The women of the second generation, those of the interwar period, evoke always their mobility through two opposing spaces: the private sphere, that of the family and communal intimacy, remains with the image of a patriarchal society their only reserved domain; the exterior world inhabited by their men and by their children represents an opening which finds them facing an impossibility: that of being able, considering the exigencies of socio-cultural survival, to transgress the family bans and the relations of inter-generational dependence.

Women of the second generation were to be naturally attracted by the French way of dressing, or even more by the extra-community leisure. Let us say that they perceived very soon two opposing worlds: the French milieu is represented as a space of liberty contrasting to the heavy atmosphere of the family cell, which in spite of its prudish silence, remains haunted by the memories of massacre.[10] But in spite of this attraction, the women remain faithful to the injunctions of a first generation which encourages them "to not forget."

In contrast to many men of the second generation, who have manifested at times a wish to forget their ethno-cultural origin as part of their unconditional adhesion to the values conveyed by the dominant culture and the veneration of French citizenship, we may say in conclusion that the women have struggled against amnesia of the past.

---

[10]On this subject see the article by J. Altounian, "Une Arménienne à l'ecole," *Les Temps Modernes* (September 1977), pp. 227-41.

The Armenian Communities of Cyprus and London: The Changing Patterns of Family Life

Susan Pattie[*]

The information in this paper is based on field work conducted between 1983 and 1990 in Cyprus and among Cypriot Armenians who moved to London. These London-based Armenians emigrated in waves: in the 1950s pre-independence and independence periods, in 1963 with the beginning of the communal troubles, and in 1974 with the division of the island.

The world is changing as it always has. The Armenian world is also changing, again as it always has. Life and culture are in motion. Armenians would be a unique group of people if we had a static, unchanging culture over any period of time or space. The last hundred years, the period on which I am focusing, has been a time of violent and often very rapid change, but it is a mistake to view pre-1915 or pre-1960s as an unchanging period of maintenance of tradition. These times were also changing.

---

[*]Susan Pattie is Lecturer in Anthropology at Richmond College and Research Associate at University College, London. Her informal remarks were taken from two chapters on the family in her forthcoming book, Faith in History: Armenians Rebuilding Community in Cyprus and London *(Smithsonian Press, Washington, D.C.)*

We often look at the variations which preceded these changes and dismiss them as individual eccentricities, just the odd person next door, but we should look at these variations to see the shifts that occurred. Armenians in Cyprus and Cypriot Armenians in London have found that surviving and rebuilding in diaspora in the last half of the twentieth century includes the shedding of many shared traits, habits, and customs. Ironically, flexibility is crucial to continuity. But what is being continued? As the community in Cyprus grows smaller, at present under two thousand people, and in London, where physical size and distance discourages immersion in Armenian activities, the responsibility for passing on particularly Armenian knowledge and language skills falls increasingly upon the family. Thus, at a time when they are least able to or likely to do it, families are being relied upon to reproduce what once the entire community worked together to create.

At the end of the last century in Armenian villages and towns, being a man or woman meant being first part of a particular extended family or *kertasdan*. While many have understood this as a patriarchal lineage system, it is very unclear just what it meant in practice. What is very clear is that, at a time of crisis, both maternal and paternal sides of the family, whichever was able, would help. Following the uprooting from the homelands, families quickly became bilateral, reckoning ancestry and closeness in both directions, the mother's and the father's side, again indicating that there was some clear foundation for this change.

The second important aspect of identity one hundred years ago was location, a particular village or town or area of the city, like Istanbul. And both in the family and the locale, women played *a* or perhaps *the* central role. But with the advent of nationalism, the rise of the intellectual, and the formation of political parties, the fulcrum of power shifted. Western or Russian patterns of modernization were followed, and with a few exceptions, women were reduced to an associate role for the most part. The dispersion also helped to unseat the women's very powerful local knowledge. The power of the network of families grounded in locality was destroyed almost entirely. The importance of the extended family of course continues today for most Armenians, but in a different form and as only a shadow of its former self. There has been a gradual replacing of the focus on family and on locale by a focus on individual work and the more abstract concept of nation.

One of the most widely believed stereotypes of Armenian life is that, until the mid twentieth century, Armenian family life was patriarchal and the rule authoritarian, both within and outside the home. This I think is not so much a reflection of the everyday workings of family life, but instead the outward face of protocol and the organized side of the community or national affairs. With rarest exceptions in these generations, men represented the family outside the home, their undisputed domain. All figures of institutional authority, except some teachers, were also male. This outer-activity structure, however, rested on the strength of the many households making up the community, and thus on the women as well as the men.

The emphasis on the importance of the home and the work within the home gave a sense of worth to those most involved in the running of it. In the critique of ethnographies of Greece, Jill Dubisch points out that the usual focus on the public realm of power relations means that women are not taken seriously as "centers and organizers of social systems." She writes: "Since domestic life tends to be devalued in Western society, and since there is a tendency both to separate the domestic from the 'real' social world and to perceive the domestic world as in some sense 'natural' and unproblematic, the significance of women's domestic roles for the society as a whole may be overlooked."[1] She goes further and suggests that in Greek households in the past, power/female was traded for prestige/male, adding that "men's public performances, rather than being an indication of their power, may be a manifestation of their lack of power in a central institution of social life, that is in the domestic realm."[2] This, I think, has also been true of the Armenian world; that is, the central and absolute importance of the home. If we accept this as true, that the home, family, and constant maintenance of family ties was a crucial factor in communal social relations, how do we know who was or is making the decisions there?

The traditional image is the submissive, perhaps manipulative wife, jumping to serve the husband, following his directions. During anthropological fieldwork, however, one observes as well as asks questions.The same questions are asked many times over in different ways and replies vary according to whether people feel they are being asked to give a social "rule" or to talk about what they personally do. Often people would tell me what relationships or actions were supposed to be, but then it turned out that this had not been the case for them. Someone would say, "This was the way it was, but then, of course, in our family it wasn't that way." Another might say, "The neighbors did it a little differently." Or, "It was that way in our family, but none of the neighbors did it that way—they were wrong." So the anthropologist finds that there was tremendous variation just below the surface of what people are giving as the self-stereotype. One

---

[1] Jill Dibisch, "Gender, Kinship, and Religion: 'Reconstructing' the Anthropology of Greece," in *Contested Identities: Gender and Kinship in Modern Greece*, P. Loizos and E. Papataxiarchis, eds. (Princeton: Princeton University Press, 1991) p. 40.

[2] Ibid, p. 44.

can guess at further variation in some of the tales and proverbs that people would tell, for example in the story that a woman in her eighties told me about wedding customs before her times. She said, "You have seen during the wedding ceremony when the bride and groom put their heads together, haven't you? Well, we used to hear, that there was a custom during that time that the bride would step on the groom's foot so that she would always have the upper hand in their marriage. '*Khoskt g'antsni*', they would say to each other. We used to hear old stories of a bride and groom stepping on each other's feet, one after the other, until the *kuhana*, the priest, had to interfere. I never saw any of this," she said, "but our parents used to tell us."

This was something that was happening before her time, at the turn of the century. The division of power and labor within each household then as it is now was not to be taken for granted. Instead decision-making seems to have rested on strength and personality, as well as particular circumstances, alongside these communal expectations of male and female roles. Segalen, who has looked at similar customs in rural France, shows how they also indicate a very loose and changing power structure within the home. Frequently in the stories told by this older generation about themselves and their parents, one hears of both men and women taking part in making important decisions, whether to move and where, who the children should marry, how to spend the household money. In many cases it seems clear that the mother was in charge.[3]

With the disruption of deportations or immigration, the domestic realm was broken apart, families dispersed and regrouped. The physical survival of the family became the

---

[3]Martine Segalen, *Power and Love in the Peasant Family* (Oxford: Basil Blackwell, 1983).

only important issue; and in numerous cases this was left to women, as men were killed or transported away. The children of these women later spoke of the great physical and emotional strength of their grandmothers, their mothers, and their sisters, who carried them through this period. This picture of the Armenian woman as possessing strong inner will and character while showing a modest face to the outside world is combined with the notion of sacrifice to the family. Traditionally the husband is to present a strong appearance of control to the outside world, including a display to the guests visiting the household. There is an element of complimentarity to these roles which Renee Hirschon brings out in her work with Greek refugees from Asia Minor (Smyrna). She portrays this as a "cooperative effort, essentially a working partnership."[4] This idea of harmonized relations was built on respect for these gender rules, but flexibility behind the facade. During my own fieldwork, many people mentioned a sense of duty as a potent motivator for married couples. An active sense of duty and respect for each other seemed a crucial ingredient for long-term marriages, and certainly some carry on with only these two as their base. But, as many pointed out, "love" is another factor growing from that initial physical attraction, to include a sense of joy of being with the other person, sharing important phases of life with him or her, enjoying the mutual support that is given. It is difficult to say where one attitude ends and the other begins, except in cases at either end of the spectrum.

Today, however, it is likely that a young couple will marry, as they say, purely for love, in the sense of a romantic, physical attraction combined perhaps with a shared

---

[4]Renee Hirschon, *Heirs of the Greek Catastrophe: The Social Life of Asia Minor Refugees in Piraeus* (Oxford: Clarendon Press, 1989).

intellectual or political commitment, or other common interests. This may take place without a sense of duty towards an extended family or community, or more than a vague idea of what one's duty towards the marriage partner might be. In earlier generations, if one was fortunate, love might grow out of this sense of duty. Today's hope is that duty and respect will grow from love. As before, this does not always evolve as hoped, but it is perhaps more difficult to maintain a long-term relationship on the basis of love alone in this romantic sense, especially when that love is rarely as unconditional as that of a parent and child. The confused sense of priorities in marriage is currently resulting in an increase in separations and divorce, but there are still few enough in Cyprus for the couple to feel isolated and unable to find others to understand what they're experiencing.

The biggest changes in the relations between men and women and between the different generations reflect congruent changes in attitude towards work both inside and outside the home. Some call it fashion, others call it education, but the attention previously given to home crafts, whether for sale or for posterity, has dwindled drastically over the last three generations in Cyprus. The birthrate continues to decrease. Girls, like their male classmates, take up an interest in secondary school which they dream of following into a career. In secondary school both girls and boys are encouraged, even pushed, to achieve high marks. A career or work orientation of education is also influenced by roles seen on television and in the movies, so that girls as well as boys come to see all valuable work as taking place either in offices, shops, or laboratories. And it is done in exchange for money. A desire for "a better education" for one's children, while fitting into one generation's general outlook, that is the one that is encouraging its young people, can work out quite differently in practice than expected. In fact, accomplishment in this sphere, usually an individual accomplishment which then reflects on the larger family, takes that individual, that person, farther away from the family, from Armenian circles, and in the case of Cyprus, away from the island itself due to the limited variety of jobs available there.

Ingrid O'Grady, who wrote about Armenians in Washington, D.C., has observed this as a conflict between the collective and the individual, where the aims of each are quite often at odds.[5] Insecurity, informed by memories of and reactions to the massacres and deportations as well as the more recent disturbances in Cyprus and the Near East, fuels the already potent concern with achievement and accomplishment. The pull of physical security towards the West, towards the development of language, business skills, and education successful in Europe, contrasts with the emotional security of the memories of Armenian community, with a sense of duty toward the past. The high value placed on relationships within the extended family can create its own tensions with these others, often conflicting directions, a problem common to many other groups of refugees and immigrants as shown for example by Hirschon, mentioned earlier, or Boyarin writing about Polish Jews, post World War II in Paris. Boyarin gives an interesting example highlighting the intellectual conflict between generations, whether as a result of different levels or kinds of education or the different historical contexts while the generations are growing up, what they have been through. He quotes an Armenian tailor in Jordan speaking to his Jewish friend, "You made a mistake, sending your son off to university, Moshe. I'm having my three sons trained as artisans. They'll come and have a drink with me at the end of day. But your

---

[5]Ingrid O'Grady, "Ararat, Etchmiadzin, and Haig (Nation, Church, and Kin): A Study of the Symbol System of American Armenians," (Doctoral dissertation, Catholic University, 1979).

son — what will he have to say to you?"[6]

Within each generation, and probably each person, there are always conflicting ambitions and desires. The striking feature is the continuity of central values passed on between generations in spite of the many outward disturbances and changes. The concept and importance of family itself receives its own reinterpretation with each new generation, but it remains at the core of Armenian values. Young people still think in terms of some kind of strongly linked family with its connection to relatives, *khnami*, and other Armenians. The security of these networks of warmth and support could also be the cushion which allows flexibility and resilience in the face of major socio-political and geographical changes.

Achievement, whether in education or career, in today's Western terms demands a more individualized view of work, one more inclined towards self-satisfaction or fulfillment for both men and women. Once viewed as a means towards an end—that is, simply supporting the family, and the extended family as well—work has become an end in itself. This increasing emphasis on individual achievement, for both male and female, creates new sorts of friction as roles evolve. The old primary sense of work within the home, the nurturing of the extended family, is gone. But at the same time, women must compete on unequal and difficult terms with men outside the home. Contemporary ideas of women as autonomous, in charge of their own bodies, compete with the traditional household of interconnected co-dependent people. Young men are also confused about their own roles and direction. Today life in Cyprus and in London revolves around the needs and demands of the job, or around the individual rather than their family. Martine Hovanessian,

---

[6]Jonathan Boyarin, *Polish Jews in Paris: The Ethnography of Memory* (Bloomington: Indiana University Press, 1991) p. 169.

writing about a similar evolution in the Armenian family in Paris, describes the shift from the collective "we" to the individual "me" as a theme of modern times.[7]

The most poignant reminders of how greatly the situation has changed are the older women living alone. Accustomed to large bustling households where the mother or the grandmother was the fulcrum of power and activity, these women have raised families and watched them leave to set up independent households. There is no longer any question of power or prestige for them, but only a bewilderment and loneliness punctuated by periodic visits. For younger Armenians, as families become more atomized, floating separately, women's powers in the home and networking between homes also becomes more limited and often more regulated by the needs of the husband's job, and in some cases the woman's own job. As outside work for both men and women increases in prestige and certain jobs require increased mobility, extended families break apart and move to different continents. In spite of these changes, studies of Armenians living in the United States and elsewhere in the diaspora consistently emphasize the importance given to family affairs and relationships. For example, studies by O'Grady, Jenny Phillips,[8] and Anny Bakalian,[9] all emphasize this phenomenon. What the family is, however, continues to change.

Once part of a large network of other families, institu-

---

[7]Martine Hovanessian, *Le lien communautaire—Trois générations d'Arméniens* (Paris: Editions Armand Colin, 1992).

[8]Jenny King Phillips, "Symbol, Myth, and Rhetoric: The Politics of Culture in an Armenian-American Population" (Doctoral dissertation, Boston University, 1979).

[9]Anny Bakalian, *Armenian Americans: From Being to Feeling Armenian* (New Brunswick: Transaction Publishers, 1993).

tions, and neighborhoods, Cypriot Armenian families in London and even in Cyprus are becoming more isolated in their own affairs. The older emphasis on the couple as part of a larger household or a unit within the community is changing to a more individual notion, one surrounded by variety and choice. The ideal mate becomes one who would make a good companion, lover, helper, and then mother or father to one's children, and much less important a link to the community and other families. Armenians in Cyprus, as in the rest of the diaspora, are defining themselves differently, new variations of the strong family emerge, more restrictive in size, less restrictive in its control of its members. In negotiating these outside changes, the family itself has changed, but the strong value its members place upon it remains.

Crossing Over to the Other Side

Martha Ani Boudakian*

My great aunt Tsainig refused to change her name when she came to the United States from Western Armenia in the 1920s. Her older brother, my grandfather, had anglicized the family name Hampartsoumian when he came to the United States several years earlier. He shortened it to Hampar, and all the other family members followed suit. With her fighting spirit Tsainig, whose name actually means "little voice" (which she has anything but), insisted on keeping her name as Hampartsoumian. She would not compromise something as precious to her Armenian identity as her name.

Two generations later my life is a different story. As an adolescent I wanted desperately to get rid of any attributes that marked my Armenian identity. I tried to remove all of my body hair, plotted when my nose job and breast reduction surgery would happen, and imagined how I would neutralize my name. I wanted nothing more than to mold the telltale signs of my Armenianness into something that just didn't stand out—into something "normal." My grand transformation also included failed attempts to starve myself and to control my volatile Armenian spirit; in short, to make myself

*Martha Ani Boudakian is a women's health nurse and has been an advocate for women in crisis. This autobiographical essay was first published in Food for Our Grandmothers: Writings by Arab-American and Arab-Canadian Feminists, Joanne Kadi, ed. (South End Press, Boston).

as little an aberration as possible from WASP culture. I believed that, despite my attempts to attain normality, I would never be good enough, because I am not made of the right stuff.

What does "normal" mean anyway? Calling something a cultural "norm" usually means following the way of those with the most political and material resources in any society. They define and impose their experience of normality for everyone. The concept of cultural norms in multi-cultural societies is historically enmeshed in power, colonialism, and control. In the United States norms are defined and imposed by white, upper class men, as they are in much of the world. Any way of life that differs from that elite, Eurocentric, and hegemonic patriarchal norm is marginalized until it is conveniently coopted by the dominant culture; even then it remains peripheral. Note the recent commercialization of Native American spiritual practices.

"Passing" for normal means trying to emulate the dominant culture, in order to survive in it. To break this oppressive cycle, we can refuse assimilation and choose what Black feminist scholar and activist Bell Hooks calls power on the margin. She cites the margin as a place of resistance where oppressed people can take what is useful from the dominant culture without adopting its ways. She clearly designates a difference between being a marginal object, forced to the edge of society, and a marginal subject, finding power to resist from the home space of the margin.[1]

Armenians have lived on the margin, both as subjects and objects. Having been dominated for so long by other peoples, Armenian diasporal communities worldwide are known for their insular cohesiveness. However many Armenians in the United States have managed to pass in the

---

[1] *Yearning* (Boston: South End Press, 1990), pp. 145-53.

dominant culture and still participate in and maintain the support of the Armenian community. On the whole Armenians in the United States have not suffered intensive economic oppression. We have shifted our value systems to accommodate the need for survival in a capitalist, industrial society by becoming literate in the language of the oppressor.

More reflective of what I understand as authentic Armenian values is the ethic of valuing people over money and material possessions. I believe that Armenian culture also encourages the well-being of the collective rather than Western individualism. Our people have an ancient and expressive literary, spiritual, and artistic tradition, connected to other Near Eastern cultures, yet very much its own. We are a lively, strong, and generous people, deeply connected to our native, mountainous land.

A critical event in recent Armenian history was the genocide of 1915 to 1923. My family and hundreds of thousands of other Armenian families endured obscene horrors during the genocide. My grandmother Garadine, orphaned at age 11, buried her own parents, then shaved her head to disguise herself as a boy in order to escape sexual assault by Turkish soldiers. She then spent the rest of her childhood at an American mission orphanage and later came to the United States as a mail-order bride.

The genocide has left a permanent imprint on the psyche of the Armenian people, one that reflects the insularity and rigidity of our communities in diaspora today. The United States appeared to Armenians, as to many other immigrants, a promised land, relatively free from oppression and full of opportunities for economic prosperity—which has become a reality for many Armenians.

Most of us refer to Armenia and other places in the Middle East diaspora as the "other side." This reference is particularly apropos in the case of Western Armenia, a life and place physically destroyed during the genocide. As a child listening to relatives refer to the other side, I thought of it as an old, backward way of living; a place that smells and tastes like *basterma*, onions, dill, and strong cognac, where everyone knows everyone else's business, where old women would persistently try to marry me to the right family. I bought the arrogant myth that Armenians had been given the opportunity to live in a superior culture by coming to the United States. In reality, for those who came here, crossing over from the other side entailed leaving one life behind for the next—a spiritual passage. The other side then became a homeland of the mind and soul that Armenians in the diaspora have strived to preserve.

I am an Armenian woman, born and raised in the United States: an American-Armenian woman. I live a hyphenated existence—two poles coexisting. Where does one end and the other begin? I function in two worlds: American and Armenian. And I am on the margin in both of these worlds. Within me exists the interface of these two worlds, yet they are very separate. Within me exists a place that is both of these worlds, merged and discrete, and a place that is neither of them. It is a place called home. It is a radical place called the other side.

A few years ago a friend asked if my childhood sense of alienation came from being Middle Eastern in an almost exclusively WASP town. I thought about it briefly and said no. Little did I know I had begun a journey I will continue for the rest of my life, a journey that has brought me home to the maze of being a bicultural diasporan Armenian feminist. The center of this labyrinth is the other side.

In the beginning was the womb of Armenian family and community, ample aunties hugging, feeding, adoring me, pinching my cheeks, and giving me big wet kisses. Huge family gatherings, with lots of noise, arguing, joy, people, and of course, food—simply the warm and unconditionally accepting space of home. I knew nothing of dissonance, assimilation, biculturalism, racism, or even sexism.

My parents chose not to speak Armenian to me and my siblings. I question if it was an active choice or a deference to internalized oppression, yielding to a desire to rear completely assimilated children. I do not envy the position of my parents. The children of recent Armenian immigrants, they grew up in the 1930s and 1940s. At that time non-European ethnicity was definitely not in. Even the mainstream trend of idolizing "exoticism" that we see today did not work in their favor fifty years ago. My parents lived with even stricter parameters defining a good American than I have. Radical identity reclamation was probably the last thing on their minds.

A generation later, I am vocally resisting what I call cultural bleach. Cultural bleach is a force in United States mainstream culture, wherein light-skinned people of color are urged to consider ourselves physically, historically, and ideologically white. Resisting cultural bleach is the refusal to participate in this kind of assimilation and is the affirmation of who we are.

From age 6, I became conscious of my family's ethnic difference. I felt proud of my Armenian identity and carried a feeling of coming from and belonging to an ancient place I couldn't touch. But on the surface, that translated to just feeling weird and out of place. The feeling of displacement grew with me. I felt a sense of otherness, yet it was amorphous, elusive. I knew where my family had originated, yet I didn't make a connection to what that meant geopolitically.

By the time I had started college, I identified as an Armenian in the sense of "being of Armenian heritage"; I was a critical outsider. What I knew of Armenian community was the stale romanticizing of the "old country" that relied on what I saw as repressive mores. I loosely participated in the

Armenian club at school but maintained my distance. I saw it as a potential social control, an unwanted chaperon. Nice Armenian girls don't admit they sleep around.

Armenian identity remained a side dish in my consciousness until I was in my mid-twenties and studying feminist theology at the Women's Theological Center in Boston. I felt more acutely displaced than ever; I knew by then that an ethnic/political/sexual/spiritual identity storm was brewing inside. And sure enough, it erupted that year. In that milieu, as well as with my renewed involvement with the Armenian community in Boston, I had the opportunity to explore identity in depth and I had the support for the upheaval it would inevitably bring.

I knew that the assumption that I, as an Armenian, am white no longer fit; I began to make the connection to the affinity I feel with women of color. Then one day at an anti-racism workshop my classmates and I divided into our usual groups of white women and women of color. Until that point we had all presumed that I would go to the white women's group. I told my peers with some trepidation that I no longer knew where I belonged. I then made a decision that changed my life. On that day, in the midst of the Gulf War, I came out to myself and the world as an Armenian feminist, as a Middle Easterner, as a woman of color.

Who is a woman of color? In her book *Cultural Etiquette*, Amoja Three Rivers defines women of color as "any [women] who have other than 'white' European ancestry. This includes: Africans, Asians/Pacific Islanders, Latinos, Middle Eastern people, Native Americans and [women] of 'mixed ancestry,' i.e. ancestry from any of the above plus white European."[2] Being 'of color' is a reference to the world

---

[2]*Cultural Etiquette: A Guide for the Well Intentioned* (Indian Valley, VA: Market Wimmin, 1990), pp. 2-3.

historical situation of European hegemony, colonialism, and cultural supremacy.

Many white women seem threatened by this identity and treat me as a "wanna be." It is as if I have defected from their camp, when I was never really an accepted member, nor did I belong there in the first place. From women of color I receive unequivocal support. I know that this process is historically and experientially rooted. It's my way of dispelling the myth that Armenians/Middle Easterners are white Europeans. In the United States we are socialized to believe that Middle Eastern identity is nebulous and liminal, or a European subculture. In actuality the "Middle East" represents a group of ancient West Asian cultures.

My political, social, and spiritual outlook on life and the world has since shifted. I am even more committed to challenging my own racism and know my responsibility to acknowledge the privilege I have. This process has transformed my colonially inspired self-hatred into self-love and pride. And it has paved the way for me to come home, to cross over to the other side.

Shifting from a generic feminist to an Armenian feminist identity also represents a profound change in the way I interact in women's community. Armenian and feminist are two sides of the coin that is myself. I now deem myself primarily accountable to women of color. Speaking and acting as an Armenian feminist, I am no longer a sympathetic and wistful outsider to struggles, groups, and gatherings of women of color, but a participant. I am not suggesting an agenda of cultural erasure in which we all jump into a melting pot. Rather, I believe that engaging in movements to bring about local and global justice with other women of color is a way of creating the other side in the present world. I honor my wise grandmothers. I honor my sisters. I honor my daughters yet to come.

I am an Armenian—strong and committed to my community of origin, as I am innovative, rebellious, and daring. Such liberation has made me even more delightfully uppity. I no longer feel obligated to explain to the dominant culture or to receive validation from it, nor do I apologize for or explain my body. I no longer want to be plastic and hairless with conical tits; I refuse to try to manipulate my body to conform to Wonder Bread standards of beauty. I feel accountable to the forces that matter; white mainstream culture is not one of them.

What does it mean to be an Armenian feminist in the United States, in the Western industrial diaspora, in the late twentieth century? To me it means, among other things, choosing power on the margin with other Armenian feminists. The Armenian women's community has begun to organize itself—Armenian feminists in the United States are beginning to gather among ourselves to discuss our experiences and how we want to mobilize ourselves as a community. Together we are expressing our commitment to our Armenian community and affirming our right to survive in a complex modern world.

In the summer of 1991, I went to Armenia. There I spent time building houses with a community of Armenian refugees from Azerbaijan. What moved me most about Armenia was being in a place where the ethnic norm was my norm—I was in the majority for the first time in my life. I found that Armenians there did not expect the crux of their Armenian identity to be some monolithic and archaic representation of "the old country." Rather, it was diverse and alive. Being Armenian was not the source of painful inferiority complexes. It just is. And yet Armenia is not the other side for me—it did not feel like home. I will not resolve my issues by boarding a plane to Yerevan. The other side is here and now.

Although the essence of this identity shift is the same, the language is ever evolving. Recently I have focused more intently on the dynamics of privilege and I am no longer completely comfortable with calling myself a woman of color, even if that statement comes with the qualifiers "light-skinned and with class privilege." I feel that I exercise too much privilege in this society to call myself a woman of color. I have experienced prejudice, but not racism. Unequivocally I do not identify as white, and I am ever searching for identity language that is reflective of our experience as Armenian women, and the affinity and solidarity with oppressed peoples I continue to express. I think this process of changing language reflects the unsophisticated rhetoric that exists to describe the politics of identity; a problem that can be worked beyond by developing our own language of identity.

I am eminently grateful to my Armenian feminists' support group for the feedback they have offered for this essay. It is due to the valuable discussions we have had about race, class, and identity that I have been able to gain fresh perspective on the politics of identity.

We are a group of about thirty American-Armenian women who meet four times a year for a day of ritual, discussion, socializing, and food. We have all expressed our feelings that an emptiness in our otherwise very full lives has been filled with the community of this group. We encourage other women to form similar groups, wishing all the joy, stimulation, and cohesiveness that we have found in these gatherings with each other. We willingly offer guidance to any similar group wishing to organize itself.

Took Hye Geener Eck? Armenian-American Women's Ethnic Self-Identification and Community Involvement

Arlene Voski Avakian*

Who are Armenian-American women? Must one be involved in community life, or speak the language, to qualify as a real Armenian? Is regular church attendance a requirement? For those who do self-identify as Armenian American what is the meaning of that identity in the United States in late twentieth century? Has their ethnic identification remained the same over throughout their lives? If it does change, what factors are responsible for that change? How does that identification as Armenian American intersect with gender? Ethnicity, like everything else, is gendered, so we need to ask not merely what it means to be an Armenian American but what it means to be an Armenian-American woman. I am in the midst of a research project to explore these issues. Using in depth interviews with women who self-defined as Armenian American, I focused on three areas: 1. the meaning of ethnicity, how these women came to think of themselves as Armenian; 2. the ways in which that identity was shaped by gender; and 3. how their ethnic identification was or was not

*Arlene Voski Avakian is associate professor of Women's Studies at the University of Massachusetts (Amherst) and author of Lion's Woman's Legacy: An Armenian-American Memoir.

related to involvement in Armenian community life.

Ethnicity, like gender, is a highly contested concept; and until very recently, scholarship on ethnicity has been based on the assimilation model. Basing their definition of ethnicity on the markers of ethnic life developed by immigrants at the turn of the century, scholars have used the measures of where people live, what occupations they hold, whether they speak the language of the mother country, attend church, or participate in other community institutions as measures of ethnicity. Treating ethnic communities unlike other cultures which change in response to material conditions, scholars froze both ethnic communities and ethnic people in time and space. The assumption was that, if the markers of ethnicity were not there, then the people had assimilated, a process that was supposed to be accomplished by the third generation. Among the many flaws in this research was the total reliance on outward behavior as a measure of ethnicity, and much of that behavior taking place in the public, largely male, space. Additionally, not until the feminist movement and the scholarship on women that resulted from it did research focus on women; ethnic men were studied and, if women were considered at all—and often they were not, assumptions were made about them based on what was known about men.

My work not only focused on the women, but was concerned with the ways in which women constructed their ethnic identities; not so much how they behaved, but what meaning that behavior had for them. The current focus on life story and narrative in both feminist and anthropological research provided a useful methodology for this project. Through in-depth interviews with a selected population I was able to explore the complexities of the intersecting identities of gender and ethnicity.

I will share with you today the experiences of two women who are part of my research. In order to protect their anonymity, I have changed their names and all other identifying markers. Both women reconstituted their ethnic identities and moved into and out of the community. One women was born into an Armenian community and spent a good part of her life deeply immersed in it, but made a conscious decision to be less involved when she was in her 40s and now, in her early 50s, is considering a move to an area where there is no Armenian community. The other woman was neither raised within an Armenian community, nor did she identify ethnically until she was in her mid 20s. She currently strongly identifies as Armenian American and is involved in work that is intimately connected to the Armenian community, yet she considers herself both inside and outside of it.

The stories of these two women are neither totally unique nor representative. I chose these women because they changed both their ethnic identification and their relationship to the Armenian community, and looking at that change reveals the process of ethnic identification. Additionally, since both of these women reconstituted their ethnic identities, they are very articulate about themselves as Armenian Americans and have also made conscious decisions about their relationship to the Armenian community. They are also very aware of themselves as women, and therefore their narratives provide us with important information about the highly contested terrains of ethnicity, gender, and identity. Theirs is a critical perspective, more critical than many of the other women I interviewed, though not singular. While a few of the women in my study felt that women were treated equally with men, most agreed that men have power over women in the community and in the family. Many of the women I interviewed who place themselves either outside of the community or on the margins cite its political conservatism, particularly with respect to women's roles, as being among the most important reasons for their distance from it.

They feel there is no place for them as adult, competent, professional women within the conservative and patriarchal Armenian community. The stories of these two women can reveal what ethnic identification means for Armenian-American women; but equally important, these narratives raise crucial issues for the Armenian-American community as a whole.

The child of immigrants, Mariam's first language was Armenian and her childhood was spent in a small town in New England which included a high percentage of Armenians in its population, though the resources in the community would not support the establishment of an Armenian church. While the town did not have a church, it was able to support a very small Armenian language school which Mariam attended, in addition to public school, from the time she was a young child through high school. Describing her childhood, she said:

> I don't remember the American part of it too much. [The town] is very Armenian. And so all our friends were Armenian . . . My father belonged to the Armenian club. My mother was very active in politics. So anything we ever did go to socially was either to an Armenian organization . . . or to friends' houses, and that was always Armenian.

Despite this substantial Armenian presence, Mariam's contact with non-Armenian children at public school made her feel that she was an outsider, that "she didn't belong," and she reports that "she felt inferior." She said, "I wanted to be more American . . . I felt like I wouldn't belong in the *odar* world." That feeling persisted into adulthood. "There has always been for me, until very, very recently, a real feeling that I didn't belong in the non-Armenian world."

When she was in high school, the family moved to another town, also one with a significant Armenian population. After high school she married "the boy next door" and began to live the life of an Armenian wife, joining her husband's church, the Armenian Apostolic church, because she felt it was her duty, and experiencing a new sense of belonging.

> I guess I went from high school, feeling as I really didn't fit in, to marrying an Armenian boy, getting very involved in the Armenian community, and feeling like—this is where I belong. And for many years, I would say about nineteen years, I was very active in the Armenian church and organization. I felt very Armeniany.

Saying that this period of her life was "fantastic," she describes an idyllic sense of community.

> The thing that I value the most—that was the best for me—was . . . the solidarity with Armenian women . . . the closeness was just very, very rich. And that was all age groups. Young mothers my age . . . and the older generation was really happy because my generation was working with them. And because I was very active, I got a lot of strokes. So it was really good me for in terms of acceptance, approval, confidence giving. That's the fantastic part.

While she describes this period of her life in glowing terms, when she reached her 40s she began to feel restricted by the community. Two decisions began a process of separation from the community that resulted in a reconstructed ethnic identification and move out of the Armenian community. First, Mariam decided to stop attending the Armenian church. She describes that decision as based on a spiritual need. She was not "tuned into the Christian part," she said. "As I look back, I don't think I was aware of it then, but some of the sexist part of the church and the intolerance I felt of other people" bothered her. She wanted a church that would allow questioning and joined the Unitarian Universalist church.

> I think that the journeys of my change started with the religious support and the type of religion that I belonged to where it encourages questioning . . . I probably joined that church because that's what appealed to me. But I probably had a lot of questions but I didn't have the support to ask them. The church validated that as well, an okay thing to do.

That decision not only started a separation between herself and the community, but also began the self-exploration she feels she continues to be involved in today.

The second significant decision was made because of a family financial crisis. The family needed another income, and Mariam went back to school to gain the marketable skills. While she was in junior college learning secretarial skills, the crisis passed. But she stayed in school and at the time of the interview had recently completed a doctoral degree. Her husband was supportive, but the reactions of the women in her community to her pursuit were mixed.

> While I really got a lot of strokes and a lot of compliments for doing it and women told me they admired me, and I know a lot did, I also used to get a few comments that . . . more of less said, don't forget either your place—don't think you're uppity or something just because you're getting an education. Or I felt a little bit that I had a responsibility to make sure that whatever I did was a contribution to the Armenian community. So I made a conscious effort to kind of distance myself a little bit from the Armenian community. And as I did that I found out that I liked it, so I distanced myself even more because from a distance what I could see was

also some of the things that I didn't like about our community.

These attempts by women in the community to keep her within the parameters of acceptable behavior for an Armenian woman had the opposite effect. As she moved away she had another perspective on her community, and she was disturbed by what she saw.

> The intolerance of other people, our ethnocentricity, and how that was reinforced by our organizations—the churches . . . I mean intolerance of non-Armenians, intolerance of different races, intolerance of sexual orientation, intolerance of people who don't fit in with the Armenian—just intolerance of anyone that is not towing the mark.

This distancing allowed her to see that she was

> always . . . interested in social issues. Even when I was involved in the Armenian Relief Society, I was instrumental in initiating projects where we would be involved in the non-Armenian community. . . . I remember having someone to speak to us about the Holocaust once and I was criticized . . . I should stick to Armenian things.

Once free of the control of the community, she became involved in projects that reflected her liberal politics, working with the homeless and low-income groups. Describing her current interests, she says, "I'm interested in racial issues. Issues in terms of oppression. Racial issues and sexism—it's a big issue in my life everyday." Central to these issues is the role of women within the community, particularly the church. Of all the things she could change within the community she

> would change the church structure and have women involved in the administration and policy-making of the church and hope that would filter down into their

everyday lives . . . with women being influenced by the church in a more positive way. I think it is a tremendous limitation on women's lives—the church.

While she did express missing some individuals in the community, she cannot envision herself going back to it.

I wish I could, but I really can't. Every once in a while I think of ways that I could—go into the community to contribute somehow, and I just don't feel like I want to put up with any of the energy-draining parts that would be there . . . I don't want the looks. I don't want the attitude. I don't want to deal with it in any way. And you have pockets of people who feel that if you're not actively involved that somehow you're doing something wrong ... I miss the individuals . . . I wish I could get back into their lives sometime.

The treatment of women and the intolerance of other people are her "only two criticisms of the Armenian community—the other stuff is good stuff."

A few years ago she described her life as having one "foot in the Armenian world and one in the American world and that is a very awkward balancing act. So what I think I have done in the last—just few years—is make a conscious choice to have both feet in the American world now."

For most of Mariam's life she was an exemplary Armenian women, yet beginning in her 40s she began to become less and less involved in the community in which she had spent her entire life and she reconstructed her ethnic identity from Armenian to Armenian American with the emphasis on the American. It is not assimilation into the American mainstream that was the cause of Mariam's decision to leave the community, but her inability to stay within the prescribed conservative values and politics that it requires from its members, particularly female members. Mariam stepped

beyond the parameters for women; and when she did, she
stood outside and saw the community from a new perspective, one that eventually became unacceptable to her.

Susan, on the other hand, moved from being Armenian in
name only to clearly identifying as an Armenian American
and being deeply immersed in work that preserves Armenian
history and culture. Susan had an Armenian father and a
non-Armenian mother. While her father spoke Armenian
and was heavily involved in Armenian organizations, he
brought none of his Armenian interests home. Attempting to
be a good wife to an Armenian husband, her mother wanted
to learn the language, but her father refused to allow it.
While the family lived very near the large Armenian community in the next town, they had virtually no contact with it.
Nor did they have much interaction with the father's siblings,
seeing them only once or twice a year though they lived in
the area. Susan, therefore, grew up knowing that she was
Armenian, but that ethnic identity had no content. Even her
knowledge of the Armenian genocide was not clear. She does
not remember exactly how or what she knew about the
genocide, only that she read some eyewitness accounts in a
book by Arnold Toynbee.

> I knew I was something called Armenian, but I didn't
> know what that meant. I really didn't know what it
> meant . . . My mother cooked Armenian food but that
> was about it.

After attending college away from home, Susan moved to an
urban center with a large Armenian community when she
was 24.

> I was sort of on a discovery road . . . I didn't know what
> kind of job I would find in [the city]. I was just sort of
> following my inclinations—one of which was to find out
> more about my Armenian side.

Susan went to one of the large Armenian organizations in the city to learn how she could connect with what was going on in the community. Trained as an art historian, she was able to immediately become part of an exhibition of Armenian arts and crafts the organization was mounting. Her attempts to create accurate catalog notes for the show were thwarted by the dearth of written material on Armenians. She connected this lack to the Armenian genocide of 1915.

> [I] had a sense about the reason why there was no information. Being a historian, I know how history is written. Someone has to write it. Someone has to document it . . . And Armenians had been doing other things. They were caught up in the genocide, so nobody felt up to it.

The immediate problem of finding information for the crafts section of the catalog was partially solved when she came upon the idea of talking with people in the community who might have information on the subject. She slowly began to understand that collecting crafts and stories from community members would be a way to document Armenian history and that it was up to her generation to do it.

> I knew that probably my generation was enough removed from it to be able to cope with it, and not only cope with the emotional aspects of it, of retelling the tales, but also have the intellectual capacity of knowing how to deal with such a project, how to organize it and make it feasible.

She began to interview people about both the crafts they owned and the skills they had learned. While she was immersed in doing this work, she had few ties to the community.

> I'd go to church dinners and stuff connected with the

exhibitions we put on, but I can't really say I felt like I was part of it. I felt bored at the dinners . . . it didn't really relate to me. I didn't mind going there and working . . . but in terms of behaving like a *hye aghchig* would behave—I mean I never wore dresses, you know. I wore my army jacket . . . I worked until two in the morning, you know, and then went home on the bus. No Armenian women would do that. And in fact, they often asked me, do you live with your parents, because they had never heard of an Armenian woman living alone by herself in [the city] or anywhere away from home.

Despite this tenuous connection to the Armenian community, her work on collecting information about crafts had a profound effect on her sense of self.

I was aware that I didn't know a damn thing [about Armenians] and I subsequently realized that there was a void in my life, and that as soon as I began learning about being Armenian, this void began to fill up . . . I felt rootless, to use a cliche. But I really did. I would wander around [the city] feeling that I had no purpose in life. That I just couldn't connect with anything. And it really felt empty, very empty. And I couldn't identify with my . . . mother's side really . . . there was nothing there. And so the knowledge of what it means to be an Armenian has really filled a big hole.

The assumption that children follow their mother's ethnic identity is clearly not true in this case, nor is the assumption that if children are not taught ethnic history or to appreciate ethnic culture it will not be perpetuated. It also seems clear that the development of an ethnic identity is not necessarily tied to a sense of belonging to an ethnic community.

An independent scholar, writing about Armenian arts and crafts, Susan feels she has a responsibility to pass on the knowledge she gains about Armenian culture through learning about these arts and crafts and through the stories people tell about their lives as they describe how they learned their skills.

> I found out so much folk culture. I found out about the kind of needlework women do, the wonderful designs they make. The illuminated manuscripts that priests make, the gardens they grow . . . I mean all those kind of things that make life meaningful . . . I said, I have to share this with everybody.

While Susan is contributing to both the preservation and dissemination of Armenian history and culture, she chooses to stay on the margins of the large Armenian community in which she now lives. Because her work is well known within the Armenian community in her city, however, she feels that community people see her as an outsider who has come back to the fold. Had a researcher studied this community she would have undoubtedly assumed that Susan was not only a community member, but a central part of it. But Susan's perspective is that she does her work "on my terms and I think they are more American terms than they are Armenian terms." Susan comments on the difference in values between herself and the community:

> I respect people as individuals, and with whatever beliefs that they have, with whatever lifestyle they have. I don't make judgments. I don't approach them with any attitudes about what I think they are, about who I think they are, or what they've accomplished or do or anything. And that's not something you find very often in the Armenian community. I mean, usually there is a judgment of people involved . . . and so to avoid that, I just make my own environment and get involved in being Armenian to the extent that I can handle.

Like Mariam, she feels that the Armenian community is too parochial, and Susan, like many of the other women I interviewed who place themselves either outside or inside/ outside the community, is disturbed by the insistence within the community that women adhere to traditional roles. Asked what she would change in the community if she had the power, Susan also focused on the role of women in the church.

> I think I would start with the women being able to become priests, since the church has such control of the community. That's the only way Armenians are going to start respecting women's gifts. So, if women were respected as priests, they would also be respected down the line.

The assimilation pattern has clearly been reversed in this case in terms of both identity and ethnic involvement. However, although Susan has reconstructed her ethnic identity as now unambiguously Armenian-American, the conservative position on women and the general intolerance of difference in the Armenian community has kept her on the margin of the community.

Had these two women been studied by looking only at what they do, we would come to some very different conclusions than the ones that are obvious when we hear from the women themselves what their behavior meant to them. We might assume that the usual assimilation process was responsible for Mariam's pull away from the community; that by leaving the Armenian church Mariam began a process of assimilation into American culture that resulted in her leaving the ethnic community and having an attenuated ethnic identity. But if we listen to Mariam's account of her life, it is clear that going to the Unitarian church was not a pull *into* the American mainstream, but a push *out of* the Armenian community. That decision provided her support for her critical questioning of the values in the Armenian community. She made a conscious decision to leave the Armenian community because of its insistence on a code of behavior that was inconsistent with the values she had developed; and those values are not necessarily part of the American mainstream. From Mariam's perspective, to stay in the community was to go against herself as a politically progressive woman. For similar reasons, Susan stays on the margins of the community, although many people in the community assume she has come back into the fold.

What does it mean when a woman who contributed many years of her life to the ethnic community feels she must leave in order to continue both her personal growth and her political commitments and when another who is making an enormous contribution to the present community and to future generations of Armenians feels she must stay on the margin of the community? These women's stories raise the question of whether ethnic communities that rigidly enforce traditional roles for women, see the world through an exclusive ethnic lens, and insist on their members' total allegiance to that perspective are actually weakening their communities rather than keeping them intact.

One of the things all of us on this panel are concerned with is silencing: silencing of difference, silencing of dissent, silencing of criticism. Mariam's and Susan's critiques are ones I have repeatedly heard in this research project as well as in an earlier one, also focused on Armenian-American women. I also heard them in the workshops I led which were attended by a variety of Armenian-American women and some men. This critical voice, mostly absent in the community, needs to be heard. I hope that by breaking that silence with telling these stories, I will contribute to opening a dialogue that is long overdue; a dialogue, I would argue, which is necessary if the Armenian-American community is going to grow and not be frozen in time.

Struggling for Life:
The Legacy of Genocide and
Armenian-American Women

Flora A. Keshgegian*

As an Armenian American and the daughter of genocide survivors, I begin my exploration with a personal reflection and what seems like a contradiction. On numerous occasions I have observed my mother, when she has been telling her story of the genocide and its aftermath, refer to herself as an orphan. At first I did not think about this self-appellation very much. I heard it simply as part of her narrative which portrayed suffering and loss, difficulties and trials. She described herself as orphaned, left bereft, and denied nurture. But in fact my mother was not fully orphaned. To be sure, her father was killed in the genocide when she was so young that she has no memory of him, and she was separated from her mother and tended by an aunt for a few years. But her mother, as well as a brother and sister, did survive. Indeed, her mother lived to be well over one hundred years old and resided in our household during all the years I was growing up. So I began to question what it meant to my mother to call herself an orphan and portray herself as such, even as an adult. Was she an orphan because she had no

---

The Reverend Flora A. Keshgegian is associate university chaplain and a member of the adjunct faculty in Women's Studies at Brown University.

father and, therefore, in a patriarchal society, no protector, no family security, and ultimately no place? Or was orphan a term carrying a broader significance of lack of relational and material nature, of being left bereft of home and homeland, and of feeling dislocated and alien? Or was its meaning something else or some combination of these?

I begin with this narrative and such questions because I see them as emblematic of much of Armenian identity, which has been shaped by a set of socio-psychological and cultural dynamics: namely, centuries of socio-political oppression and occupation, culminating in massive genocide; followed by Turkish denial and "allied" betrayal; and by exile/emigration and life in diaspora for many Armenians. I propose that this peculiar heritage has bequeathed to Armenians a legacy of trauma which remains largely unresolved. As a result of this lack of resolution, those of us who struggle to make change in Armenian society do so in a psychosocial environment textured by this traumatizing history. Further, Armenian-American women may well find ourselves in a particularly contradictory and difficult position. In western patriarchal cultures women are often expected to uphold and transmit tradition and cultures; we are expected to be the conservators of heritage. But what does it mean to conserve and transmit a legacy of trauma? When we try to alter the terms of relationships and to change definitions, to construct a different culture and identity as women, we so often find that we are experienced as threatening and we are marginalized or rejected. It is in this complex and difficult terrain that Armenian American women try to plant and nurture hope. But such hope cannot blossom unless the legacy of trauma is recognized and resolved. Otherwise, our histories will continue to plant seeds of destruction which will choke any delicate plantings of hope.

Because many Armenian Americans live out in our families, as well as in our communities, the legacy of the genocide, I would suggest that our lives have often been ones of such planting and choking. There are few Armenian-American families not directly touched by it. At the time of the genocide, the great majority of Armenians in the world lived in the Ottoman empire.[1] The vast majority of survivors emigrated, many to the United States. There were some, such as my paternal uncle, who had emigrated prior to the events of genocide and so escaped them, but they often had family left behind. Additionally, many of these emigrants married survivors.

This impact continues today. For example, in an informal survey I conducted at the July 1993 gathering of a group of Armenian-American women, the twelve women present claimed among themselves thirty family members who were survivors of the genocide. Most of these were grandparents, a few were parents. The furthest family relationship was greataunt and greatuncle.[2] The genocide and its legacy often comes up in discussions in this group. It is also a frequent topic addressed in Armenian publications and other forums. Clearly the genocide is a community preoccupation; its legacy lives on among us.

Given this shared experience, I want to consider the effect of these historical realities on the well-being of Armenian people, and more specifically the effect on Armenian-

---

[1]Levon Boyajian and Haigaz Grigorian make the same point. See "Psychosocial Sequelae of the Armenian Genocide," in *The Armenian Genocide in Perspective*, edited by Richard G. Hovannisian (New Brunswick, NJ: Transaction Books, 1986), p. 183.

[2]This group of women, to which I belong, define ourselves as Armenian-American feminists. We have been meeting in the Boston area since January 1993 to explore together our experiences as Armenian-American women. We represent different levels of involvement in the Armenian community as it is constituted in America and contain among ourselves numerous other differences as well.

American women. Due to the limitations of this format and the state of scholarship on these issues, my exploration will be general and preliminary. Using psychological theory about trauma, which I find illuminating in relation to the dynamics of genocide and its aftermath, I will survey the present impact of the three legacies indicated above: namely, the personal and social psychological legacy of oppression and genocide, the political legacy of Turkish denial and "allied" betrayal, and the cultural and political legacy of living in diaspora and having whatever "homeland" remains, up until recently, a part of the Soviet Union. I will also consider the implications of these dynamics for women in particular and suggest a point of departure for further exploration.

Trauma, as a psychological phenomenon and dynamic, represents a particular approach in psychology. Most psychological theories treat mental distress and its attendant symptoms, such as depression and anxiety, as pathology and illness or as manifestations of deviance. Correlatively, psychology has sought to heal the patient or socialize the deviant. Trauma, however, is neither illness nor deviance. It is injury. Judith Herman, a psychiatrist and author, states: "Psychological trauma is an affliction of the powerless . . . Traumatic events overwhelm the ordinary systems of care that give people a sense of control, connection, and meaning."[3] The sequelae of trauma, which seem to be symptomatic of fragmentation and disorder, are to be understood as attempts to adapt and to cope with the injury and its attendant distress.[4]

---

[3]Herman, *Trauma and Recovery* (Basic Books, 1992), p. 33.

[4]Post-traumatic stress disorder describes the condition of those who have been subjected to traumatizing experiences. Thus far most of the attention paid to PTSD, as it is called, has been in relation to soldiers' experiences in war and in relation to domestic and sexual abuse. Some attention has also been given to the

Trauma, especially in instances of abuse or violation, is caused by victimization, which involves coercion and injury. Victimization is an action or event, perhaps repeated over time. It is something that is done to or happens to the victimized person, in relation to which she is able to exercise little freedom or control. However, as psychologists and researchers working with those who have been abused have observed, sometimes, especially in cases of repeated abuse, those who are abused will internalize the victimization and develop a self-identity as victim.[5] Herman suggests that, in instances of repeated trauma, what she labels a state of captivity, the result may be "the creation of a willing victim."[6] Ironically, that identity may be the result of learning behaviors that practice a form of resistance and so enable survival. For example, in the case of child sexual abuse, practicing dissociation may allow a child who is being continually assaulted not to feel the horror of what is happening to her. But later on, as an adult, if she dissociates whenever she feels insecure or is approached sexually, she will preclude her ability to make a choice and will continue to be victimized in these situations in which she actually has

---

experience of political prisoners and those tortured. PTSD was officially listed as a mental disorder by the American Psychiatric Association in 1980 (Herman, p. 28).

[5]Herman suggests that this process may be reinforced when the symptoms are not recognized as related to trauma: "This constraints upon the traumatized person's inner life and outer range of activity are negative symptoms . . . With the passage of time, as these negative symptoms become the most prominent feature of the post-traumatic disorder, the diagnosis becomes increasingly easy to overlook. Because post-traumatic symptoms are so persistent and so wide-ranging, they may be mistaken for enduring characteristics of the victim's personality" (Herman, p. 74-75).

[6]Ibid.

more freedom of choice. If the original trauma is not dealt
with and if the identity as victim is not actively confronted,
these dynamics will continue to perpetuate themselves in
the individual person, and also in families and society.
Trauma is then not only a psychological, but a socio-political, phenomenon. New generations will inherit narratives of
trauma and victim identity and will be schooled in behaviors that play out the identity. As Herman states: "Denial,
repression, and dissociation operate on a social as well as an
individual level."[7] Indeed, victims are not born, but made
and re-made in changing circumstances. Victim identity
may be communicated, assigned, and constructed within
given societal contexts in order to serve certain dominant
interests. Those assigned the identity often continue to live
out and pass on the role of victim. Change necessitates
transformation through a process of recovery.

Recovery from traumatizing and victimizing events
happens as those events are recognized as involving trauma
and they are worked through.[8] Such a process involves
much struggle and pain; it requires safety, a supportive
social context, and "witnesses"—others who will hear and
acknowledge the trauma.[9] The work needed to be done for
full recovery is not possible as long as those who have been
traumatized are still struggling simply to survive or do not
feel sufficient safety, trust, and security to take the risks of

---

[7]Ibid., p. 2.

[8]Herman contends: "Remembering and telling the truth about
terrible events are prerequisites both for the restoration of the
social order and for the healing of individual victims." (p. 1).

[9]Ibid., p. 8-9. Herman also discusses the tendencies to forget
and to cover up, which serve the perpetrators' interests. She sees
witnessing as a moral stance; it is not an action of neutrality. (p.
135).

recovery.[10]

Applying these perspectives to Armenians, the original traumatizing events were centuries of political repression and social discrimination, followed by genocide. Those historical realities victimized and traumatized many Armenians over time. While those traumatizing events are long past, the legacies of injury, of denial and betrayal, and of diasporic displacement and alienation still impact the dynamics of recovery.

Further, this legacy of trauma is not only a present reality for the survivors themselves, but for their children and descendants. Indeed, it affects Armenian society and culture. Yet we have done little to examine this trauma and its implications. Compared to the work that has been done in the Jewish community about psychological issues for survivors and children of survivors, very little has been done in the Armenian community. It has only been in the last twenty-five years or so that serious attention has ever been given to collecting oral histories and doing basic studies.[11] Few workshops have been held and even less written on the experience of children of survivors. What emerges from the little that has been done is precisely a legacy of trauma and the internalization of victimization, not only for survivors, but for their heirs. This legacy manifests, among other ways, as feelings of insecurity, lack of safety, sadness and shame, a negativity toward life, and feelings of helplessness.[12]

Given the need for witnesses, the political legacy of

---

[10]Ibid., chapter 8.

[11]Major effects include the oral history project of the Zoryan Institute (Cambridge, Massachusetts) and Donald Miller and Lorna Touryan Miller's book based on oral histories, *Survivors: An Oral History of the Armenian Genocide* (Berkeley: University of California Press, 1993).

[12]See Boyajian and Grigorian, pp. 177-85.

Turkish denial has reinforced the trauma and had lent a particular character to Armenian recovery. The Turkish government and its official pronouncements and agents, including many Turkish scholars, have consistently denied that any genocide took place. Despite eyewitness accounts and much other evidence pointing to the reality of genocidal activities, Turkey persists in such denial. My aim here is not to argue the Armenian case but to point to the effect on the Armenian community of this ongoing denial. Armenians are still trying to get a hearing for our cause and to attain some acknowledgement of these "crimes against humanity."[13] This situation is further compounded by a history of Western equivocation and betrayal. After World War I, the Western Allies did little to protect the Armenian people.[14] Meanwhile, the American government refused a mandate to protect the young republic of Armenia which had declared independence after the war; since that time the United States has courted Turkey as a strategic alley and has been guided by either isolationist, economic, or defense interests.

As a result of these historic circumstances, a great deal of energy has gone and continues to go into proving the genocidal case and establishing reliable witnesses. Responses to this ongoing denial also often have a reactive quality. I believe these political dynamics tend to reinforce the victimization and make it difficult for Armenians not to think of ourselves as victims still.

Another factor affecting the legacy of trauma is that

---

[13]Marjorie Housepian claims this term was coined by the French in reference to the Armenian genocide. See her article "The Unremembered Genocide," *Commentary* (42:September, 1966), pp. 57-58.

[14]When Turkey began a counter-offensive after its initial defeat in 1918, the Allies within its borders withdrew and left the remaining Armenians defenseless.

many Armenians live in diaspora. Up until three years ago, except for the years 1918 to 1920, Armenians have had no independent republic or nation for hundreds of years. The psychological, social, and political implications of diasporic existence are multiple and complex. For example, central concerns include issues of security and of insuring a future, of establishing leadership and of defining identity.[15] Diasporic existence lends a particular weight to feeling different and alien in the dominant culture, as well as feeling threatened in one's identity and even continuing existence. Individuals and groups seem caught between, on the one hand, the lure of assimilation as a remedy for alienation and, on the other hand, the threat of assimilation as a potential betrayal not only of one's Armenian heritage but of those who suffered and were killed. Given Gérard Chaliand's definition of diaspora as collective memory and his observation that "diasporas draw from a disaster as the matrix of their collective memory," forgetting and betrayal are clearly linked.[16] As a result, for Armenians in diaspora, letting go of the history of victimization, resolving the trauma, may seem as if one is selling out to the host culture, on the one hand; while the cost of holding on to such a legacy perpetuates feelings of insecurity and alienation, on the other.

Add into this complex mix of trauma and its legacies the factor of gender difference and the picture gets more complicated still. The dynamics of trauma and victimization and the

---

[15]Related to these concerns and issues are such questions as the following: Which are the central community institutions? How is the culture to be formed and preserved, transformed and carried on? What does it mean to be a people with only some of the land which contains much of one's heritage?

[16]Iskhan Jimbashian, "Memory of the Skin: Gérard Chaliand on the Geopolitics of Cultures," *Armenian International Magazine* (4: August 1993), p. 15.

legacy of threat and violation may affect Armenian-American women in particular ways. The distinct experiences of women during the genocide and after it, such as rape or forced marriages to Turkish men or the assumption of family leadership roles after the departure or death of the men, have been especially understudied.[17] At this point, we have few resources available for examining women's experience of either victimization or survival.[18]

Further, as Eliz Sanasarian has indicated, "the female survivors in the post-genocidal era were additionally subjected to patriarchal and ethnic norms."[19] Concerns for communal survival reinforced the existing patriarchal structure of Armenian society through arranged marriages and female submission to the needs of the family. Also in the diaspora, the church, which embodies and supports the patriarchal ethos, has served as the central institution in the community.[20] As is often the case in the church and in such

---

[17]See Donald E. Miller and Lorna Touryan Miller, "Women and Children of the Armenian Genocide," *The Armenian Genocide: History, Politics, Ethics*, edited by Richard G. Hovannisian (New York: St. Martin's Press, 1992), pp. 152-72. The Millers argue that women and children suffered more during the genocide because most of the men were killed early on. Based on oral histories, they offer a survey of the range of suffering and experiences, but do little critical analysis. Typically, rape and the threat of rape are mentioned, but the impact of the trauma is not explored. There seems to be a reticence to discuss such concerns, including among the survivors. See also Eliz Sanasarian, "Gender Distinction in the Genocidal Process," *Holocaust and Genocide Studies* (4:1989), pp. 449-61.

[18]Principally available are narrative accounts: fictional, biographical and autobiographical, including oral histories.

[19]Sanasarian, p. 459.

[20]Given the political structure established for minorities in the late Ottoman Empire, the church was the central institution there as well, and clergy were the community leaders.

patriarchal communities, though women are the backbone and workers in most endeavors, they are often silent and silenced about their own opinions and needs. Many will talk about Armenian women as strong, few of these women will claim power or be seen as powerful.[21] Women's concerns are rarely discussed.

Another aspect of post-genocidal diasporic existence is seeing success, by the standards of the culture of diaspora, as proof of one's survival. For women this has often meant adaptation to the norms of American society which includes not only sexism, but racism and classism. Survivor narratives often portray America as the promised land of opportunity and salvation. These texts sometime construct a particular set of relationships in which Armenia is weak, America is strong, Armenians are needy, Americans are generous, etc.[22] Or else they portray Armenians as better, but needing to "play along" with the culture in order to have a place in it. These texts and the subsequent history of immigration and acculturation also reflect particular definitions of difference

---

[21]Arlene Avakian makes this point in "Armenian American Women: The First Word," *Transforming the Curriculum: Ethnic Studies and Women's Studies*, edited by Johnnella E. Butler and John C. Walter (Albany: State University of New York Press, 1991), pp. 271-301. I would also point out that in the genocide women were more often survivors and had to display strength, cleverness, ingenuity, and power in situations in which they felt powerless. They also used resources to survive in situations they could not necessarily change. Perhaps given this historical inheritance, we need to think in more complex ways about power. See, for example, Elizabeth Janeway, *Powers of the Weak* (New York: Alfred A. Knopf, 1980).

[22]For a treatment of such issues in Asian missions, see Kwok Pui-lan, "The Image of the 'White Lady': Gender and Race in Christian Mission," *The Special Nature of Women?* edited by Anne Carr and Elisabeth Schüssler Fiorenza, *Concilium*, 1991:6 (London: SCM Press Ltd., 1991), pp. 19-27.

which reinforce the racist, sexist, and classist structures of power and privilege in America. They need to be analyzed for the particular ways in which they obscure and obfuscate the dynamics of trauma and reinforce particular constructions of women's role and identity.[23]

Thus we Armenian Americans have a complicated history of experienced trauma and an inheritance of transmitted trauma and adaptive coping mechanisms. Where does that legacy leave us as Armenian Americans and as women? It leave us, I think, somewhere between trauma and recovery. According to Judith Herman, the process of recovery from trauma begins with the establishment of safety, moves on to remembrance and mourning, and then on to reconnection. I will attend briefly to each of these aspects of recovery in relation to the situation of Armenian Americans. While Armenian Americans often do not feel safe in the world, the reality is that most of us are relatively safe. There is no immediate threat, especially for the children of survivors, who are less likely to be plagued by nightmares and other intrusions. Feelings of lack of safety, for women especially, originate more from a sense of powerlessness than from danger. It is important that we be able to discern and

---

[23]See Arlene Avakian, "Who's Calling Who an Ethnic and Why? Women, Ethnic Identification and Community Involvement," unpublished paper: "Ethnicity as articulated within the hegemony of the United States has capitalism, patriarchy, and white supremacy at its core and therefore analysis of ethnic groups must look at the ways in which the group is positioned in relation (sic) the resulting social formations."(p. 4) Based on interviews of Armenian-American women, Avakian concludes that most of these women "feel there is no place for them as adult, competent, professional women within the conservative and patriarchal Armenian community." She further argues that "Armenian-American culture is both patriarchal and white supremacist and is not seriously challenged from within or by the larger hegemony on either issue." (p. 25)

nurture feelings of safety, as well as differentiate ways in which we actually are not safe from ways we are. We, especially as women, need to claim the power to act in the world.

It is through the work of remembrance and mourning that recovery proper progresses. As Armenians, while it seems that all we do is remember and, some would say, we dwell too much on remembrance, I would contend that we have not remembered enough in a way that can be healing. Our remembrance has taken form in a range of responses. Some have faced the past with silence and will not speak of all that gone before.[24] Given the relatively recent practice of recording oral histories, it seems we accepted the silence for a long time. Yet even the silence is about keeping hold of the memory, albeit by burying it. Other forms of remembrance focus on lamentation or a kind of chauvinism. Lamentation recites a litany of suffering and pain and speaks repeatedly of all that existed before, of all that has been lost. Chauvinism leads with a pride that extols Armenians as superior and tends to remember the suffering by a defiant reaction to it. Emphasis is put on the heroics of survival. The messages I received from my family and from my culture were a contradictory mix of a chauvinistic pride that scripted Armenians as better than other people and a recitation of all that Armenians had suffered and do suffer. I see both these dynamics, however, as responses to the experience of trauma and its aftermath. Though Armenians have tried to resolve the trauma by chauvinism or lamentation, neither has

---

[24]Dorothee Soelle, in *Suffering* (Trans. by Everett R. Kalin, Philadelphia: Fortress Press, 1975), writes of mute suffering: "Extreme suffering turns a person in on himself completely; it destroys his ability to communicate." She suggests that only belief in the possibility of change will bring a person out of silence (p. 89).

worked, especially for women. The chauvinism has a conservative quality which demands that women fit into traditional roles; it tends to limit our freedom. Lamentation has a repetitive quality that keeps the future closed. And as Leonardo P. Alishan points out: "Lamentation can console but can't conceive."[25] It does not bear new fruit. In effect, both of these forms of remembrance are reactive and are rooted in fears of loss.

I would argue that none of these schematized and formulaic narrative approaches is adequate for remembrance as Herman intends it. Remembrance of victimization for her is about facing into the abuse and violation, seeing it fully, and naming it for what it is. As I have already indicated, that process of telling needs to be heard and witnessed. But in the process the victimized person also needs to sort out and tell for her/himself the "truth." Part of the goal of remembrance is to come clear about victimization, but not victimhood, to recognize the ways Armenians in the genocide and its aftermath suffered, but also to see what Armenians did to survive and how they exercised agency, not necessarily in a heroic sense or because they were better than others, but because they were capable human beings who wanted to live. There are many amazing stories of actions, little acts of agency, that made a great deal of difference. As we claim those with due pride, self-perception may change. Such moments of agency are difficult to claim, however, or even to recognize, if we are caught in some other scheme, such as lamentation focussed on suffering, or chauvinism focussed on idealized heroics.

Additionally, the process of remembrance for healing involves mourning. For all the lamenting we have done as a

---

[25]See "An Exercise on a Genre for Genocide and Exorcism," in Hovannisian, ed., *The Armenian Genocide*, p. 346.

community, I am not so sure that we have ever truly mourned. To mourn is to recall all that has been lost and to grieve, to feel all the pain and hurt and then let go, to let the past be the past. The past will only stay in its place and be given due honor if we do indeed mourn. To be sure, our ability to mourn has been made more difficult by the factors I have indicated, by the lack of reliable witnesses and by the dislocation of diasporic existence. Yet without the mourning, we seem to vacillate between lament or boast/bravado, in a way that may console and/or posture, but does not conceive or change or heal our community.[26]

After the mourning comes the reconnection, which is about integration within ourselves and with others in community and culture. Acceptance of the injury and injustice can free and empower. It enables one to take responsibility for creating a future and reclaiming the world. That reconnection indicates that we have moved on to a new place; and while the past is not forgotten and indeed its remaining scars will remind us time to time of what went on before, that particular past will not dominate our lives. I think we have often resisted reconnection because we saw in it the potential of being lost in a sea of assimilation. Yet reconnection does not have to mean that. It can include reconnection to the rest of our own history which itself is obscured by the genocidal landscape. For us as Armenian-American women, it can also mean new ways of understanding ourselves and positioning ourselves in society.[27] To accomplish those changes, we need to attend to a process of recovery from trauma and develop new narratives that do not reinscribe

---

[26]Herman points out: "Mourning is the only way to give due honor to loss; there is no adequate compensation." (p. 190).

[27]Herman sees as central to reconnection the adoption of a "survivor mission" and the pursuit of justice in a broader arena (p. 209).

victimization, that do not transmit the trauma, that do not simply brag or lament, but that do enable us as daughters to work through our inheritance for ourselves and for the honor of our mothers and foremothers.

So I come back to my mother's naming of herself as orphan and the orphaned hope that seems to haunt the self-understanding of Armenian-American women. In my mother's narrative, her mother is rendered invisible and non-existent by the claim of orphanhood. Yet, I would suggest, that if we, as women, are to narrate our lives differently, a fruitful place to begin would be with relationships among women. We need to attend to the ways in which we understand and construct relationships of mothers and daughters, grandmothers and granddaughters, etc. How do these relationships socialize women into a legacy of trauma and into the dominant culture? How do they contain and communicate resistance and transformative affirmations? Indeed, just such attention is evidenced in recent literature by Armenian-American women, such as Arlene Avakian's autobiography, *Lion Woman's Legacy: An Armenian-American Memoir*,[28] and Carol Edgarian's novel, *Rise the Euphrates*.[29]

It is for us, the daughters, to hear and tell our mothers' and foremothers' stories anew, in a way that perhaps they themselves could not or cannot, but which names them not only as orphans or victims, but effective resisters and agents of transformation. That process of re-telling requires a different kind of attention to their stories, a different relationship in which we serve as witnesses as well as heirs, in which we examine literary schemas for their narrative intent, their limitations, and their possibilities. This work also calls for a critical political consciousness and a reexamination of

---

[28]New York: The Feminist Press, 1992.
[29]New York: Random House, 1994.

the politics of genocide and recovery, diaspora and national/ ethnic identity, in order to understand the ways in which portrayals of Armenian women have been used to serve certain interests and maintain social arrangements which uphold Armenian society as patriarchal and which do not conflict with the dominant American culture. Claims to women's agency and power are resistant readings in both cultures, which go against the grain of cultural expectations. They are subversive; they are sub-versions.

Returning again to my mother's narrative, while I understand her need to tell her story of victimization and trauma, I want to tell the story anew so that the victimization is recognized but not reinscribed. I also want for myself as an Armenian American to recognize and nurture that orphaned self which exists in us in such a way that we can fully claim hope. As I have indicated, that process of coming to hope requires that we remember and mourn the suffering and loss and let it go. Letting go is about risking and stepping out and creating new places to stand and to position ourselves anew. So I conclude with another story about my mother. My mother emigrated to the United States at the end of World War II, and she had to take a rather circuitous root from Beirut to Cairo and the Sudan, Dakar and Lisbon, Newfoundland and finally New York. During these travels, she had to negotiate her way, as well as take care of two young companions who traveled with her for much of the time. Whereas her orphan narrative is a recital of what was done to her, her journey narrative tells of what she did to accomplish her voyage and the voyage of these children. In recalling that story, I want to affirm my mother's courage and agency and to reclaim hope for all of us as women of power, on a journey to a new life.

Armenian-American Women Inhabiting Out Bodies: Engendered and Embodied Ethnicity in Carol Edgarian's *Rise the Euphrates*

Janice Okoomian*

We live in the age of what is called "multiculturalism" in the United States. To be white and ethnic, sometimes even to be a person of color, is fashionable. This is true not only in the culture at large, but also in the academic fields of American literary and cultural studies, where the intersection between race/ethnicity and the female body is a popular subject for research. Most scholars who write about this topic, however, have focussed on what it means to be a woman of color in the United States. It is only recently that research is beginning to pay attention to white women's bodies.

Armenian Americans are one of many white ethnic groups in the United States, but we are too small in number to command much public attention or political power; thus we are not a fashionable object of academic scrutiny. Nonetheless, I believe we can make an important contribution to feminist and American studies by looking at the power dynamics (both gendered and racial) that intersect in the Armenian-American female body.

Janice Okoomian is a doctoral candidate in American Civilization at Brown University.

The subject of my paper is Carol Edgarian's recent novel, *Rise the Euphrates*, which I believe can tell us much about the current condition of Armenian-American women. Before I begin to talk about the novel, let me give a brief explanation of the ways that literature can help us understand culture. In an earlier era of literary studies, it was popular to think of literature as a reflection of, or a response to, reality. However, in keeping with literary and cultural theory of the past twenty years, I favor a more complex model, in which the text and the culture in which it is written arc part of a larger system of knowledge called a "discourse." I am using a Michel Foucault's widely known definition of discourse here: a set of rules, conventions, and practices which both enable and set limits upon knowledge and which permeate a wide array of cultural institutions.[1] For instance, when we talk about the female body we might talk about such topics as the differences between femaleness and maleness, the relationship between the body and the mind, or the similarities and differences between the human body and machines. The conventions of the discourse guide us toward these topics and away from others. In other words, the discourse makes some things visible and others things invisible. The most basic premise underlying this interpretive strategy is that all forms of identity are culturally con-structed, rather than innate, and that they are always being produced and reproduced by cultural institutions, art forms, relations of power, and language.

What does this mean for our reading of *Rise the Euphrates*? Because the novel is part of the United States discourse on the female body, our interpretation will consider not only how the female body is represented in the text, but also how the

---

[1] This definition is only a partial one, but sufficient for the purposes of this paper. For a more complete definition of discourses and their properties, see Foucault's *The Order of Things* and *Archaeology of Knowledge*.

text is actually producing or defining the category of the female body. We will pay especially close attention to those things which the text makes invisible.

The novel begins by narrating the genocide survival story of the protagonist's grandmother, who is called Casard. After witnessing the torture and execution of many members for their village at the hands of the Turkish soldiers, she and her mother are force-marched to the Euphrates River, where all the remaining villagers are expected to drown themselves. But Casard lets go of her mother's hand at the last moment; she survives the genocide, but from that time on cannot remember her true name. Taking this as a sign that she has betrayed her mother, Casard looks to her descendants to heal the past. Her daughter Araxie, poisoned by the legacy of guilt and death, tries to escape that legacy first by marrying an odar, George Loon, and later by having an affair. So it falls to Casard's granddaughter, Seta Loon, to recover Casard's true name. The novel explores how each of the three generations confronts the dilemmas of Armenian-American ethnicity and femininity: they must come to terms with the genocide, legitimate their voices, and learn how to be female in an American context. In each case the struggle enacts itself through things that happen on and to the bodies of these characters.

Because literature represents the world non-visually, we must rely upon language to understand how the bodies are gendered and racialized/ethnicized in *Rise the Euphrates*. Attention to language about the female body in this novel reveals an abundance of oral references—lips, mouths, eating, feeding, are all prominently figured. We also see descriptions of physical pain, focusing on bellies, veins, and, again, on mouths. These images have everything to do with the problems of Armenian-American female identity.[2] Let us consider three sample passages from the novel in which lip or mouth imagery is employed. In these excerpts, the three central female characters are linked in a nexus of trauma, voice, and fashion.

In the first passage, Casard and Araxie are so closely identified with each other that they seem almost to be one individual:

> And their breath. It smelled the same, a combination of lamb, pekoe tea, mint, and bananas. It mattered not the men they were with, or the children, or how high in the community they might scale. They had the same breath. As a young girl Araxie watched Casard apply her makeup and experienced the odd sensation of her mother's methods and intentions, and yes, the ghosts of the Euphrates, too, planting themselves like a pair of lips on Araxie's white bones. In such moments, it was possible for mother and daughter to find communion and ease, with themselves and each other. (55)

The use of breath as a figure in this passage is symptomatic of the novel's central if implicit assumption that the bond between mothers and daughters is innate. They have the same breath because of the genetic bond between them, and because they engage in similar physical behavior, namely, they eat the same foods. Their physical bond is a precondition for the metaphorical link between their voices; actions of the conscious mind, such as their arguments over the choices Araxie makes, may disrupt but cannot obliterate the physical bond. This scene also reveals why Araxie's life is so tormented. Casard applies makeup, and through this act

---

[2]Orality is perhaps the central problematic of Armenian-American femininity, as it is represented in the text.

inscribes the legacy of genocide upon her daughter.

Casard tries repeatedly, through arguments as well as through ritualistic acts such as the lipstick scene we just looked at, to make Araxie obey her. Araxie doesn't obey her mother, but is deeply affected and develops an identity crisis. In the second excerpt, Seta as narrator tells us that Araxie's

> troubled soul only heightened her outward beauty: her black swath of hair, her deep pooled eyes, the lethargic ease with which Momma made even the smallest gesture seem infinite. Countless mornings I stood beside her to watch the wand of her lipstick slowly, painfully describing the O of her mouth. (4)

As we now see Araxie applying makeup herself, it is clear that each time she traces the outline of her mouth with the lipstick, she is freshly defined as Casard's daughter and as the one whose inheritance is a past full of death and torture.

A third scene completes what I call the lipstick trilogy in the novel. In this one, it is Seta's turn to apply lipstick to her mouth, sitting alone at her mother's vanity:

> I unrolled a lipstick and applied it; in recent years, Momma had begun to favor pink shades of lipstick, with names like Cordelia and Gypsy Rose. I glanced into the mirror. This is what she sees. This. (272)

Again we see the mother-daughter bond (wearing Araxie's lipstick, Seta is able to see her mother in the mirror); Araxie's recent taste for pink lipstick suggests she is trying to look younger, perhaps to return to a time in her life before the conflict with her mother overwhelmed her. The romantic, slightly risque names of the lipstick colors (Cordelia, Gypsy Rose) suggest that Araxie is trying on different ways of being feminine and sexual. Significantly, it is immediately after putting on the lipstick that Seta discovers evidence of her mother's affair. The impact of the genocide persists, we are thus to understand, into the second and third generations. Because the characters are so closely identified with one another, it seems not at all strange that the genocide affects them all. By the end of the novel, Seta heals the wounds of the past through discovering her grandmother's true name, making peace with her own mother, and getting pregnant, thus ensuring the survival of the family into the next generation.

In part, the progression of lipstick through the generations follows the assimilation formula of most white ethnic American literature: the first generation, the immigrants, cannot fully adapt to the new world ways and desire at all costs to transmit the culture of their country of origin to their offspring; the second generation, caught between old world ways and new world ones, rejects the former; it is the already assimilated third generation that goes back and reclaims the ethnic identity. William Boelhower, a prominent scholar of ethnic literature, argues that immigrant novels look nostalgically at a golden past in the mother country, bemoaning the loss of authenticity in the present.[3] Here Edgarian departs from the formula followed by most white ethnic literature, as she must in order to account for the hellishness of the Armenian past that precipitated Armenian immigration to the United States. Edgarian rightly shows that the impact of the genocide upon our lives makes assimilation difficult for Armenians, but assimilation is clearly an imperative imposed by American culture on its white immigrants.

In the novel, I believe assimilation tension underlies the lipstick scenes, as well as the numerous references to other modes of orality—people eating food, sucking lemons, kissing,

---

[3]William Boelhower,"Ethnic Trilogies," in Werner Sollers, ed., *The Invention of Ethnicity* (1986). Sollers and others in the Ethnic literary school make similar arguments.

playing the duduk. What should we make of the orality of Armenian-American culture as depicted in the text? The novel seems to lend itself to Freudian interpretation, which would go something like this: cut off in the most horrific imaginable ways from the nurturing of our mothers, Armenians never progressed beyond the oral stage of infant sexuality. The novel's main project would then be to move Seta beyond that oral stage and into adult (phallic, heterosexual) sexuality. And in fact this is exactly what happens in Part II of the novel, which is called, appropriately, "Kiss Me," and is devoted to Seta's adolescence.

But there are two problems with using Freudian theory to interpret the novel. In the first place, there's a Eurocentrism to the Freudian perspective. Like members of other colonized groups, Armenians are infantalized and assumed to be somehow less developed than supposedly more advanced Westerners. We are lulled into forgetting that most Western cultures are the colonizers, rather than the colonized, and they have the luxury not to have to contend with massive psychological wounds such as those inflicted on the Armenians by their colonizers.

The second problem with the Freudian reading of *Rise the Euphrates* is that is makes certain troubling assumptions about femininity and sexuality. I said at the beginning of this paper that novels, as elements of a discourse, make some things visible and other things invisible. I am critical of Edgarian's reliance upon genetic and mystical ties to explain what Casard, Araxie, and Seta all have in common, because I believe in doing so obscures the cultural, social, and historical forces that shape these characters. So let us now uncover what the novel makes invisible about Armenian-American women's femininity and sexuality.

In order to negotiate this central problem of how to integrate Armenian and American cultures, Edgarian's female characters must undergo an acrobatic set of bodily contortions. I have used the lipstick scenes here because I think that the beautification process transacted through the lipstick rituals is not at all value neutral. How is it, for instance, that Casard, who resists intermarriage, processed foods, and drip-dry fabrics because they are too American, uses lipstick, which is certainly not an Armenian fashion? And what does it mean that it seems so normal for her to do so, that we can read about it without, so to speak, batting an eyelash? Resistant as she is to some elements of American culture, I argue that she has readily embraced American notions of femininity, and that the novel's attempt to portray her as unassimilated masks the ways in which she does conform.

Araxie's struggle to negotiate Armenian traditions and American culture has even more dire consequences for her body. The varicose veins she inherits from her mother, for example, gesture to the Euphrates swollen with genocide victims. And in Seta's narration about watching her mother apply lipstick, Araxie appears to suffer physically through conforming to the disciplines of Western fashion. But the exoticization of her beauty in that passage shows that she has already been positioned according to American ideals of feminine beauty, in which what makes her beautiful is her difference from European norms and the suggestion of suffering that marks her as a descendent of a tragically doomed, eastern culture. The term "Orientalism," coined by Edward Said, can help us evaluate Araxie's status vis-a-vis American culture. Said tells us that Orientalism is a Foucaultian discourse, "a Western style for dominating, restructuring, and having authority over the Orient,"[4] and he points out that Orientalism "view[s] itself and its subject matter

---

[4]Edward Said, *Orientalism* (New York: Random House, 1978), p. 3.

with sexist blinders . . . women are usually the creatures of a male power-fantasy. They express unlimited sensuality, they are more or less stupid, and above all they are willing."[5] All American readers, whether we be female or male, descended from Eastern or Western cultures, are accustomed to orientalizing the bodies of Eastern women. Edgarian plays to this bias by stressing Araxie's exotic beauty and promiscuity.

The text's project to incorporate Armenian women into American norms of femininity and sexuality culminates in Seta's attitudes and behavior. Seta is repulsed when she glimpses Casard's legs: "blue like a river, purple as a bruise, veins crisscrossed her white, white skin, soft as a baby's."[6] I have already suggested that the veins signify the Euphrates, and indeed part of Seta's revulsion is horror at viewing a sign of the tortures inflicted by the Turks on the Armenians, but we must not forget that this scene of revulsion is enacted over the female body. It was, after all, women who were driven to the Euphrates, it is women who get varicose veins in childbirth; the rivers of fluid within their bodies threaten to rise (as the book's title tells us). In short, the Armenian woman's body represents femininity gone amok, and it must be contained by the disciplines of Western fashion. Only then can it be safely displayed and exoticized.

Araxie understands that the game of Westernizing the Armenian woman's body has high stakes. In one last lipstick

---

[5]Ibid., p. 207.

[6]P. 143. This passage invites a closer scrutiny of the way racial categories are being produced through the Armenian-American women's bodies, and indeed that is an important element of my reading of the novel. We need to address not only the fact that the Armenians are white in the United States, but that their mode of whiteness differs from what we usually think of as white. Sadly the limitations of scope prevent me from addressing this question more fully here.

scene, she seeks out an orphan girl, perhaps a stand-in for her orphaned mother, and searching her purse for a gift, pulls out keys, lipstick, a comb, and a roll of candy. All of these are offered, and the child, wishing "to make the correct choice," picks the lipstick. For Seta, this knowledge comes more dramatically when her friend, Theresa Vartyan, is abducted by a milkman, who rapes her, beats her, and then leaves her for dead. Armenian orality, we are to infer, makes us vulnerable. Theresa expresses her Armenian difference through promiscuity and flamboyant clothing, and although the novel sympathizes with her freedom of spirit, her story is a cautionary tale from which Seta must learn.

To conclude, let me suggest that what Seta has at stake, we all have at stake. I believe that *Rise the Euphrates* accepts the terms offered by American culture to Armenian-American women. The novel conveys the message that, although we might have some difficulty inhabiting our bodies in the way American culture wants us to, it is a good goal to strive for. Thus, the novel implies that we accept conventional femininity (heterosexuality, makeup rituals, and so forth) as normative. But to do so we must repress, erase, or at the very least tame those aspects of our femaleness which mark us as different.

The Armenian Women and Social/Political Innovations: Opportunities and Reality

Ludmila Harutunian*

If we ask ourselves which word is used most frequently in Armenia today, we will find that it is the word "change." We have seen change, we are undergoing change, and we are awaiting change.

During the past several years, the Armenian flag has been waving along with more than 150 other flags in the world and it makes us feel proud. And, taking this opportunity, I want to congratulate ourselves on the occasion of the establishment of the independent Armenian state.

But allow me to therefore go on to the question of what has changed in Armenia as a result of this. There have been changes in the internal demographic structure of the country, and Armenia is still undergoing change in the economic, political, and social sphere. Positive answers will give birth to hope, but negative answers are certainly discouraging.

For me there is no choice. Armenia must be independent and must exist. Democracy means first of all equal opportunity for all, for women as well as for men.

Let us attempt to understand the level of women's equality. I must share with you sociological data because I

Ludmila Harutunian is chair of the department of Sociology at Yerevan State University and a member of the Armenian Academy of Philosophical Sciences.

am a sociologist. All of the data emanate from a recent poll taken by the sociology department of Yerevan State University and are quite representative.

To the question as to whether you believe women and men are equal in Armenia and whether they deserve the same rights and opportunities, we received the following answers: 40 percent of the women and 54 percent of the men answer that God himself created men and women unequal, and therefore society cannot give them equality. If they are unequal, it is God's fault! Then, 43 percent of the women polled and 37 percent of the men believe that society must create equality in order to alleviate or prevent social tension; 17 percent of Armenian women and 9 percent of Armenian men believe that it is through the efforts of women that the world will become beautiful and we will come out of this difficult situation. As you see, only a small portion of the population believes in and recognizes the equality of women.

When we speak of equality, we are talking about women's hopes, and it seems to us sociologists that, if women are not equal in society, perhaps they are equal at home. We assumed that perhaps there was a division of roles in society so that in the public realm it is the men who rule and at home it is women who rule.

And so we asked about the contemporary family in Armenia. A total of 19 percent of Armenian women and 50 percent of Armenian men agreed with the statement that the man is the "lord" at home and women must serve as exemplary home economists and managers. Then, 54 percent of Armenian women and 43 percent of Armenian men responded that the Armenian home is an egalitarian institution in which men and women make decisions together. Finally 26 percent of women and 7 percent of men said that the women run the home. Note the difference in the evaluation of women and men. They are the women and men who live in the same home.

But the data also show that there are serious changes taking place in the home, changes that the Armenian men do not want to see. But women know very well about those changes because they have made them. If we rely on this data, then we must have hope. Because in the Armenian home it is the women who teach the children. And I believe that those Armenian women who believe that women are equal to men will teach their daughters and their sons in such a way that the future Armenian home will become truly egalitarian.

Armenia is at the edge of the world, at the intersection of East and West. Until now we have been inside a very large country, the Soviet Union. Wherever that country has gone, we have gone as one. And that country was going towards the West, slowly, but it was heading that way. When the Armenian state was created, we were faced with a choice: which way to go. We want to appear European, we want to be similar to the West. But let's take a look at the direction in which the changes of the last three years have taken us.

The relatively low level of women's participation in government has been well presented here at this conference by Hranush Hagobian. I have tried to look at the causes for this situation. And it has become clear that one of the reasons is the negative public opinion regarding woman leaders. In our poll we asked whether there should be women leaders in Armenia. Further, we asked whether it is possible to hold simultaneously the concepts of woman and leader. And we received a very sad response. Nearly 50 percent of respondents said that it is not possible to use the terms woman and leader together. And approximately 50 percent believe that yes, indeed, women can be leaders. And I want to tell you that women's opinion on this issue is much more conservative than that of men. A total of 40 percent of Armenian women, but only 34 percent of Armenian men, absolutely exclude the possibility of the existence of Armenian women leaders. But there remains a small hope.

Some of the respondents offered their opinion that women have lots of energy, so they should become leaders in order to use that energy; 25 percent of the respondents agreed with that statement. Other respondents said that women leaders and the twentieth century are synonymous, and therefore Armenia must have some women leaders in order to appear to be a democratic country; 13 percent of the women and 25 percent of the men had that response. Another response was that women leaders are essential, that they are a force of power that will help us; 7 percent of the women and 8 percent of the men hold this opinion.

But let us try to understand whether men are unjust or unfair in their approach towards women or whether there are bases for this attitude. Sociological data shows that today Armenian women are much more conservative than men. Our society is in general a conservative one, but women are more conservative than men.

When we asked, "What is your response to the changes that are taking place in Armenia today?" more women than men say that the collapse of the Soviet Union was a great misfortune. More women than men do not want privatization of the economy. More women want to rely on government rather than on themselves. Fewer women want to find for themselves political work. The following question was posed: there is unemployment and at the same time there are a certain number of jobs; who should get those jobs? Women say, men should. That is the reason women do not want to become leaders by and large.

So therefore we can come to the following conclusion: that, yes, it is true that there is not a very receptive feeling today towards Armenian women leaders, but women themselves are responsible to some extent for the formation of that attitude.

We should also ask whether it is easy to become a female

leader in Armenia today? Armenia is living in difficult times. The population believes that the problems facing the nation are greater than the problems facing women and that it is not possible to solve both sets of problems simultaneously. There may be some justification for such an opinion, but my fear is that the attitudes of society might diverge so far from the ideals of equality and rights for women that it may be very difficult in the future to come back on course regarding the position of women.

Let us look at the implications of not dealing with, not talking about, the problems of women. Women face greater unemployment than men. Women face greater poverty. The problem of poverty has become a problem of women. Women feel this problem in a more intense way because it is women who have taken on themselves the problems of the family. We have asked health related questions and it has become a pattern that women's subjective evaluations of their health are much lower than those of men. Women feel they are sick. Women feel that they are tired, aged. That opinion has no objective value except that it shows a person's psychological inner feelings, their sense of self, which is the most important criteria to judge the quality of life.

Can you picture the situation in the Armenian family, where children constantly see their mothers in a condition of feeling either ill or tired all of the time? Women believe that the opportunities of employment for them are much more limited, and the status implications of that feeling are serious.

Let me say that I make this report with a great deal of sadness and pain. But I have no place to say this except in a forum such as this, among other women.

In answer to the question of whether you are proud to be a citizen of an independent Armenia, the response was the following: 61 percent of Armenian men said yes, but only 50 percent of Armenian women replied in the affirmative. I am convinced that there are many more who are proud to live in independent Armenia. I am personally proud. But we are talking about thousands of women. And then the question was posed: if you had the opportunity to leave Armenia, would you leave? Only 29 percent of men and 33 percent of women said, yes. There is a small shred of hope there. This was a question of opportunity; we were not asking whether a person is prepared to leave Armenia, we were talking about the possibility. But I want to call your attention to a much more serious result.

We examined these figures by generation and found that 17.5 percent of those under the age of 25 said, yes, they would leave; 38 percent of those between the ages of 26 and 40 said the same; 27 percent of those between the ages of 41 and 55 said, yes, they would leave; and only 9 percent of those above the age of 56 said that they would leave. But we are convinced that Armenia has a bright future and the women gathered here today are working that future. And if the younger generation wants to leave Armenia, I don't believe that the Armenian nation will benefit.

I want to conclude with the characteristics of the ideal Armenian woman. When we conducted research in 1990 (we regularly conduct studies on the concept of the ideal Armenian woman because that gives us an idea of the direction in which society is moving), we received the following picture: that the ideal Armenian woman was intelligent, strong-willed, devoted, polite, beautiful, caring, and obedient. This result in 1990 gave us a great deal of hope, because it provided as the ideal a picture of a working, active woman. And there are many present here who would have approached that ideal.

Today, in contrast, the following qualities in women are valued: moral, noble—30 percent; modest—29 percent; beautiful—28 percent; hardworking—17 percent; intelligent—15 percent.

And men's image of the ideal woman gives the highest values to the following qualities: modest and humble—37 percent; of good morals—35 percent; beautiful—31 percent. As you can see, the mind has disappeared from this list. I want to point out to you that this is a change towards conservatism and plainly reflects the direction that exists in Armenia today, that is to return a woman to the family and to render her the humble, obedient wife and mother.

I would not focus on these issues if woman leaders were not sitting here today. It seems to me that we must return home after this conference anticipating problems and talking about solutions to these problems.

Today, in this arena, radical changes are not possible. The society is living in difficult times and great responsibilities are faced by women. The same change is taking place in all republics of the former Soviet Union. But it is essential to stimulate and to aid the development of an active women's movement in Armenia. It is important to talk and to conduct research about women's problems.

And it is essential to call people's attention to the fact that women and men have equal rights in society and are, after all, children of the same nation.

Creating a New Agenda for Armenian Women

Violetta Aghababian*

The end of the Cold War has inspired a hope to many people for unprecedented progress in the social-economic sphere. But this is not the time of miracles, and the problems which have been plaguing the world community still exist. Moreover, these problems have become more frightening for the newly independent states. Unemployment, especially among women, poverty, crime, interethnic violence, and civil conflicts are the topics of our major concern. The social-economic crisis leads to the loss of considerable material and cultural values accumulated during this second half of the century. This directly refers to Armenia. Her fate is a matter of our special attention, and this is the major reason for this reunion.

Armenia, against her will, has become an experimental area for the world community. This is a land where human possibilities are under probation of emergency situations. I must agree with some scientists who state that Armenians have developed a genetic code of adaptation to extremely unfavorable life conditions. Now is the time for an all-Armenian struggle for national renaissance, which should begin with the improvement of living conditions for Armenian

*Violetta Aghababian is the secretary-general of the Armenian National Commission for UNESCO at the Ministry of Foreign Affairs of the Republic of Armenia.

women.

Women are the mirror of the society. Today we can state, without exaggeration, that Armenian women represent the hardships and misfortunes, difficulties and achievements, hopes and disappointments of our nation, which, in this century, endures the third, historically new, stage of the formation of her statehood.

In this process the social condition of women as well undergoes a transformation, which is reflected mainly on their work and education. In spite of long controversies and a number of legislative acts, the condition of women, in almost all the countries of the world, compared with that of men, is inferior. Inequality of the sexes still exists practically in all the spheres of human life.

But in Armenia, especially before 1989, we had a different situation. This was probably conditioned by a high level of education and by the absence of inequality of sexes in the entrance examinations to higher educational institutions. In accordance with the data of the last census of the population in 1989, out of the 3.3 million population of the Republic, 51 percent are women, 68 percent of them live in cities, 649,000 women have jobs, and more than half of them have higher and secondary-professional education. About 10,000 women are research workers, more than 2,500 of them are doctors and Candidates of Sciences. Today, about 70 percent of the medical doctors and teachers and 30 percent of the engineers and economists of Armenia are women.

As far as salary is concerned, unlike many countries in the world, in Armenia its amount is determined by the position, and inequality of sexes in this sphere has been also lacking.

The devastating earthquake of Spitak, the long-lasting military conflict in Karabagh, and the resulting blockade of land transport and energy crisis, the destruction of decades-old relations with the outer world, the abrupt decline of production—all these difficulties, which have burdened one small Republic, have not by-passed the spheres of science, education, and culture.

The lack of central heating interrupts the educational process during the winter months. Irregular transportation schedules and expensive fares have prevented rural students from regular attendance in classes. Shortages of material resources, equipment, and raw material have created numerous difficulties for the development of science. This results in the loss of competitiveness in international research projects. In this respect, the assistance provided by the International Science Foundation to Armenian researchers, who are ranked fourth among the scientists of the former Soviet republics, should be mentioned.

Thus, out of 456 grants of the Soros Foundation donated to Armenian researchers, ninety-seven have been received by women, making this number 21 percent of the total. Unprecedented low life standards of the technical intelligentsia, who receive a salary equal to two to three U.S. dollars per month, naturally hinders the development of science.

As science requires excessive effort and time, the roles of each in the family becomes more significant in assisting women scientists. In this regard, the education of young boys acquires utmost importance in preparation for family life in the spirit of mutual respect for mothers and wives.

Since its foundation, UNESCO has always concentrated its efforts upon the humanization of interrelations between men and women, as well as improvement of women's conditions. In progress is the analysis of the mechanisms influencing violence caused by scarce family income.

Since 1992, Armenia has been a member of UNESCO. For more than two and a half years the Armenian National Commission for UNESCO has been established. Within its structure the Committee on Women's Problems is functioning, which creates new possibilities for Armenian women to be involved in international affairs and effective cooperation. In November we are scheduled to host a UNESCO seminar on women's problems in the post-communist period. Participants from eleven CIS republics will take part in the seminar, which is preparatory to the 1995 Women's Conference in Peiking.

The Armenian National Commission for UNESCO has prepared a complex program on health/nutrition education in primary-secondary schools, which will make effective use of Armenian national folklore, puppet theater, youth theaters, and mass media. Special lessons will be dedicated to the purpose of formulating respectful attitudes in boys towards women and the idea of equality.

We have just published the Armenian translation of the book *Human Rights, Questions and Answers* by Leah Levin. The book also contains problems on women's rights. I am honored to present this book to you during this conference.

The basic natural vocation of women is maternity. 60.6 percent out of the total number of Armenian women aged 18 and older are married, 10.4 percent are widows, and about 5 percent are divorced. The Armenian family is one of the most durable in the world. For each one thousand population, nine marriages are registered annually. Out of one thousand marriages an average of five married couples are divorced. Out of one thousand people, approximately twenty-three babies are born. But this data does not show the realistic situation of the country, it does not include the statistics of the consequences of the earthquake and the Karabagh conflict. I refer to the dead, the invalids, orphans, refugees, and migrants, the overwhelming majority of which are male. The consequences are very serious.

Today we note a tendency of a decline in the birth rate (81,192 births in 1986 compared to 70,581 in 1992) and in marriages (31,465 in 1986 compared to 22,957 in 1992). We are worried about a comparatively high rate of mother and infant mortality. All the aforementioned testify to the necessity of a complex scientific examination of the consequences of the three misfortunes which Armenia faced during the recent five years.

Without this it is impossible to organize social assistance for women, children, families, and the entire population of the Republic. In this respect, young families, and particularly young mothers, are in need of a special attention. The following data about the natural nutrition of babies may furnish important information to highlight the problem. In 1988, for example, 64.4 percent of Armenian babies were breast fed during the first years of life, in 1989 this figure was 59 percent, in 1990 it was 57 percent, in 1991 it fell to 47.6 percent, and in 1992 it fell even more to 37 percent.

This is a troubling statistic which illustrates the difficult situation of the young family. I consider it a matter of social utility to realize two long-term nationwide charity acts under the motto: "Young family" and "Health of women is the health of the nation."

It is noteworthy that, if in the Armenian family there is an active process of equalization of matrimonial relations, in the political sphere and governmental level we observe a tendency of excluding women. This requires enhancement of women's activities in Armenia. In this aspect, the comprehensive support of women's organizations, as well as of different categories of women, particularly soldiers' mothers, female teachers, and single mothers, is highly desirable. In my opinion, it is time to establish a Research Center for Women's Problems in the Republic. I propose to elaborate a document concerning the organization and the structure of that Center. The project could be submitted to UNESCO for evaluation and further intellectual assistance and partial financial support. We could begin with the establishment of an International Foundation "Armenian Woman." I wish great success to the Conference and benefit to our motherland.

Women and Local Government

Jemma Ananian*

I will be discussing women in government in general and in local government in particular. I would like to discuss the statistics that have been presented during the past two days concerning women's representation in government, both on the local and on the federal level, in Armenia. Note that the percentages of women representatives have not simply declined in recent years, but have fallen dramatically. I'd like to point out the problems that women face in Armenia, and the tremendous barriers that women have to overcome in order to take on powers or positions of leadership.

I do not accept the explanation that the depletion of numbers of women represented in our government is due to the fact that people look down upon women in power or in leadership roles. In fact it is painful for me to hear it said that women should not be in power or that they do not wish to hold positions of power. Philosophers have observed that history would go forward ten times faster if people did not crush the intelligence of women.

This situation can be explained in the following way. I have worked under the old system and now under the new conditions of our democratic and independent republic. Formerly women were assigned quotas, so that at least 55

---

*Jemma Ananian is mayor of the town of Ijevan and a member of the Parliament of the Republic of Armenia.

percent of all representatives in government were women, whether workers, members of the proletariat, or doctors. Their work or profession did not matter; however, there were quotas.

In 1959, when I was first elected to office, 37 regions were represented; and in each of these 37 regions, women were represented, so that out of three secretaries, one was a woman. Thus, in 37 regions, there was leadership and representation by women. And even if a woman was to step down for one reason or another, she was replaced with another female in order to show that women do have the same rights as men.

In the Constitution of the old system, there was a provision which stated that men and women enjoy equal rights—rights to education and work and the professions. However, the Constitution specified equal rights and not equal responsibilities. While women and men were placed on an equal footing outside of the home, within the home the woman bore the obligations of being a mother and a home-builder and carried complete responsibility for the running of the household. As a result, the duties of being a homemaker crushed the ability of the woman to become as hard a worker or as capable a professional in the outside world. It is this dual responsibility carried by a woman that makes it much more difficult for her in comparison with a man.

The new beginnings of our country as an independent republic have been very difficult. The situation has been particularly harsh for the vulnerable members of society as a result of a number of problems—economic, financial, the energy shortage, the lingering consequences of the 1988 earthquake, to say nothing of the blockade of our country and the six-year-old war. We must therefore ask the following question: is it not the case that the first victim of the current circumstances in our country is the woman? That the current hardships are crushing the heart and the soul of our women?

Thus, during the elections, if in the past when I ran for office I received 94 percent of the vote, I do not believe that the same would be true today. This is because of the changes that have taken place, because life is more difficult, because the things that a woman could accomplish in the past she cannot accomplish today. Recently a friend came up to me and said, "Jemma, I am asking you to do some things, and I know you can do them, because I have known you for many years and you have always been helpful." But I had to reply to her, "I can not." Circumstances in the country today have changed, and the changes are influencing women in different ways. The consequences are that women will not win the votes as they would have in the past because their morale has been hit hard.

I am heading the local government in Ijevan, which has 100 kilometers of common borders with Azerbaijan. This means basically that my region has been at war for the past six years. I wondered therefore, when I came to this conference and saw the agenda and program, about the fact that no one was discussing the effects of the war on woman. Don't think that only my region, or the war zone, is being affected by the war. As a result of the fighting, the heart and the soul of the woman is being broken. This is true for the entire region, all of Armenia is going through the same experience.

We have many victims in our region. We have more than seventy fighters who have died in the war. Equal to that we have seventy women who have been killed in the war, in a peaceful manner while they were sitting in their own homes, watching television or simply working in their gardens.

The number one wish that we all share is that peace will come to the country and the war will end. But even after peace does come, there are major consequences that will remain. There are orphaned children and orphaned mothers.

While we are suffering from the consequences of war, however, in the meantime we are very thankful and proud of all those people around the world who understand our pain and suffering, explain the situation to others, and spare no cost in providing us with assistance. I thank you all.

Basically Armenian women continue to carry the spirit of the Armenian national hero Vardan Mamigonian, who saved the nation in the fifth century.

We return then to the question of whether women should take powers of position and leadership? And the answer in my opinion is that women not only should, but they must do so. Women have a kindness of spirit as well as the ability to serve their people and their nation. And the strength of a woman, according to the Armenian legend of David of Sassun, is the strength of a lion. Whether the lion is male or female, a lion is a lion. Therefore women can come to positions of power like a lion.

I wish all of you every happiness as a woman. I wish for you the kindness and the strength to remain Armenian, whether in the homeland or in the diaspora. And I am convinced that, no matter how far apart our roots may spread, in the end our branches will come together and meet.

Women in Science and Literature and the Educational System

Bella Saroukhanian*

The role of science, as well as literature, and the arts, is obvious in our life. Development of sciences makes our life more comfortable, if it is used for peaceful aims. Good literature and art make our life more beautiful.

The participation of women in both fields is important. It is in a woman's nature to become a wife and mother, to bring up her children as good citizens of her country and for the benefit of the globe. This brings the woman very close to her main role—that is the continuation of the mankind, which needs continuous protection of mankind from wars and misfortunes.

If we look back in history, it becomes evident that not always and not in all countries is it possible for a woman to play an active role in the development of science and culture, let alone diplomacy. Speaking generally, we can say that in Western countries there were and there still are more possibilities for a woman to participate in the development of science and culture than in the Eastern ones. This, of course, is not true for all countries and for all periods. And the division of countries into Western and Eastern ones is, very often, symbolic.

*Bella Saroukhanian is a member of the faculty of Romance and Germanic Philology at Yerevan State University.

In the 1920s Armenian woman began to play an active role in the cultural life of the country. This role became more active during and after World War II. Beginning in the early 50s the role of women in culture became more creative. Today it is as fundamental as the role of men.

The picture is more interesting in the sciences. Changes here take place faster. According to the statistics, the number of women doctors in arts and history as well as in medical sciences is increasing today. By the way, the percentage of educated women in Armenia is the largest for all the republics of the former Soviet Union. The reason for this change is, in some cases, education. Though the educational system in Armenia has had many problems and can be criticized, it gave us the opportunity to have such positive results.

But today, unfortunately, this process is growing backwards. The unbearable conditions under which our scientists work and educate the younger generation, the lack of new information, the impossibility of communicating with our colleagues from other countries—let alone practicing abroad—may make one think that science and culture in Armenia is lifeless. But there is one ray of hope. We know our problems, for sure. This means that we must and can plan to make definite changes in it. And for this we must work together, support each other, and make a program of how to return life to science and culture in Armenia. Now I'd like to look at the Higher Educational System in Armenia and the problems that exist there, problems that we encounter every day, the consequences of which can be very sad unless we don't act right now.

The Higher Educational System in Armenia is a rather constructive one today. We have two universities: Yerevan State University and the Polytechnical University. One more has been added: California University or American University of Armenia (AUA). In addition we have one conservatory for musical education and seven institutes. They are: Institute for the National Economy, Pedagogical or Teacher's Training Institute, Institute of Foreign Languages, Medical Institute, Institute of Theatrical or Fine Arts, as well as Veterinarian and Agricultural institutes. During the last two to three years a number of private universities came to augment this list. So the quantity of specialists we prepare is more than necessary. But what about the quality? It is decreasing day by day.

I'd like to take as an example the Faculty of Romance and Germanic Philology, not only because I teach there, but also because the great majority of the staff and students here are women. Lessons here are possible only for six months instead of the previous ten. (I am sure the picture is the same in all other higher educational institutions.) The reason for this is lack of electricity and heat in the winter.

We may say that these are factors we cannot control. They are the result of blockade, and so on and so forth. And this is true. But let us consider the consequences. The students become indifferent to their classes and research work. Thus, despite a very high level staff, we don't have the expected results. So on the one hand, today's student is a potential director, or member of government, or some kind of manager in 10 to 15 years. There is simply no other choice. And on the other hand, the possibility of undertaking research work for the staff is minimal for economic reasons and for the lack of contact with the outside world, and with it an absence of fresh information.

I hope that women here are not naive and that we will recognize the problem of education as among the very important things. Today we have many problems that are considered to be of first-class importance. The best title to be given to these first-class problems we have in Armenia is, perhaps, "how to survive." These are the problems concerning health, food, electricity, etc.

But the key problem today is that of education, of how to have highly intelligent, educated young people. If we do not consider it to be a key problem now, later we shall suffer from the lack of intellectual leaders. So my suggestion is that we work together, organize discussions and inquiries, find ways out, and thus coming to conclusions and make final decisions. I think we have to make a project of the following:

1. how to find out talented young specialists among the army of very smart specialists (by the way more women than men, because men generally are able to find their own path even through the thickest forest, and besides all these organizations are to solve problems of women),

2. to support our specialists to use their brains maximally and sponsor them to conduct research work outside of Armenia,

3. to undertake research work and acquire experience in the countries where this or that field is on the best and strongest background. In other words I claim to have a unique educational program for our nation, having the support and sponsorship of all of us living both in Armenia or the diaspora for the benefit of New Armenia.

Women and Health:
An International View

Isabelle Valadian, Marie Farrell and Matthew Higgs*

INTRODUCTION: ONE WOMAN'S STORY

The door to the shabby hospital room was closed as we approached. A tall, thin, slightly bent man in equally shabby clothes stood near the door looking exhausted and apprehensive. Dr. Victoria and I entered the sparsely furnished room and stopped. Our eyes were riveted on the woman in the bed. Ashen grey. Motionless. One single intravenous line in her arm. She looked about 65 years of age. She was 40.

The woman opened her eyes and began to speak in the local language. She said her husband was a good man. This was not his fault; but they could not take care of any more children. Dr. Victoria's body became tense and her eyes hardened. She listened and then told me the woman's story.

The woman and man lived in the mountains outside the capital. She tried to abort a pregnancy and began to hemorrhage. She and her husband walked for twelve hours to get to the hospital. Dr. Victoria added that the woman's physical condition was tenuous. Her nutritional Ostatus was extremely poor, she was obviously anaemic, and had lost a good

*Isabelle Valadian, M.D., is Professor Emerita, Harvard School of Public Health, Department of Maternal and Child Health. Marie Farrell, M.D., is Adjunct Professor of Nursing, Harvard School of Public Health. Matthew Higgs is an Editorial and Documentation Consultant.

deal of blood.

The woman and her husband had eight children, ages one through 18. With her history and health status, the woman's prognosis was not good. Dr. Victoria was not optimistic for the woman's survival. In this Eastern European country, there is no contraception or education about birth spacing. Abortion is against the law.

After spending some time with the couple, we sat outside and talked of Dr. Victoria's years of experience. Looking straight ahead, she said, "I don't care what they say. *I* have seen the women. I have in front of me the eyes of all the women who have died from those policies. It has to stop."

Dr. Victoria, like many others, recognizes the resilience these women maintain. She also recognizes the assaults the women experience throughout their lives which deprive them of the energy and stamina needed to survive. And some don't. And many, while they live a few years longer than men, suffer with chronic illness and disability which significantly diminish the quality of their lives. As for Dr. Victoria, she remains today an agent of change. Her country has moved to more humane family planning policies, and she is partly responsible for those changes.

This story focuses on three factors that we suggest are keys in understanding the rationale for health policy related to women's health and in making the changes needed to enhance and promote women's health: the resiliency of women, women as a disenfranchised group, and women as agents of change.

THE RESILIENCE OF WOMEN

The first element that Dr. Victoria's story underscores is the strength of this Eastern European woman, a characteristic we submit is common among all women in the world. They bounce back from physical and emotional hardship. They are *resilient*. And they share the same legacy as other women throughout history who have managed against all odds to survive, *and* to be productive.

WOMEN AS A DISENFRANCHISED GROUP

What else do women worldwide have in common? Most if not all have been *disenfranchised*. They first recognize that some thing or some event is at odds with their personal experience. Importantly, they are able to feel the difference, label the difference, and question its meaning. They are able to acknowledge the discrepancy between what their intuitive sense suggests and what they were told was the way things are. And they rejected what they were told. They say, publicly, that some things have to be put right. They will not accept the policies, practices, and regulations which prevented them and other women from growing and developing fully.

Dr. Victoria lived the nightmare of fatalistic family planning policies. She knew from her studies and from her clinical experience that women's bodies could not sustain the repeated assault of one pregnancy after the other. Despite a country's need for people, or wish to populate its rural areas, or economic need for manpower, the resources of women were not for public consumption.

Somehow Dr. Victoria and these women know implicitly that if some things do not change, women will fall behind, they will get sick, and they will die. Ultimately, they recognize that even for the resilient, there are limits to the physical, emotional, social, and environmental assaults which anyone can endure and still survive. They learned these things, not from the law, but from their studies and from their experience. From living. From watching their mothers produce more children than their bodies could tolerate. From watching their sisters married off to men twice their age and totally indifferent to their needs as mere children. From helping friends cope with AIDS and care for their family at the same time. From seeing too many women beaten by men, and from watching their mothers, abandoned by their fathers, work as cleaning women *and* still manage to send their children to the best schools money can buy.

WOMEN AS AGENTS OF CHANGE

But Dr. Victoria and women like her are different. Because they were not sensitized to these events, they made up their minds that they would *do* something about them. In short, the experiences transformed them, and they became *agents of change*. They chose their avenue and their venue. Some became nurses and worked through the health system, some became engineers and worked through the environment, and some became teachers and worked with children and families to ensure a different kind of human experience for women.

But regardless of the approach, the message was and is the same. Deep down, women and men know the strength of women. Deep down, all recognize the necessity of strong, competent, resilient women in a changing complex world. And while much remains to continue the process, it had to begin. And it has been women, agents of change, who have launched the effort.

PURPOSE OF THIS PAPER

In this paper, we suggest that three elements are needed if the chances for women's optimum growth and development are to be improved. First, knowledge of the physiology and physical characteristics of women provides the foundation for decision-making. Second, given the assumption that women worldwide demonstrate an enormous capacity to endure, or to be *resilient*, sensitivity is needed to recognize those situations in which the biological bases and gender differences between men and women are ignored or, in some instances, violated, situations in which women have been disenfranchised. Finally, we assert that those who possess this knowledge and are sensitive to the issues must become agents of change if the chances for women's survival and quality of life are to become a reality.

A CALL FOR CHANGE: A WORLD OF WOMEN TALK

The agents of change have been vocal. They demanded and got ten years of attention through the United Nations Decade for Women, 1975-1985. During this period they called a world meeting of women. To talk women-talk. To come to terms with the issues that Dr. Victoria and millions of women worldwide experienced. And to tell everyone that the new world order happened to include women. They spelled out the changes in documents which represent, on a global level, what every woman knows on a personal level. They called these efforts the Nairobi Forward-Looking Strategies.[1]

INITIATIVES ON WOMEN, HEALTH, AND DEVELOPMENT (WHD): A GLOBAL PERSPECTIVE

The UN Decade for Women firmly established the special health needs of women and their role in community participation.[2] First, the World Health Organization (WHO) defines health as a state of physical, mental, and social well-being, and not merely the absence of disease or infirmity.

THE NAIROBI FORWARD-LOOKING STRATEGIES

All UN member states committed themselves to the Nairobi Forward-Looking Strategies and passed World Health Assembly Resolution WHA 39.18 for the health sector.

---

[1]The United Nations, *Women, Health and Development: The Nairobi Forward-Looking Strategies* (Copenhagen: European Regional Office, World Health Organization, 1984), chapter 1.

[2]Director General's Progress Report to the 40th WHA on Women, Health, and Development (Geneva: World Health Organization, 1987.

The Director General's report in 1987 to the World Health Assembly proclaimed that "if the inequities in women's health are not redressed, there will be little progress toward the goal of health for all."[3] In response WHO coined the term, "Women, Health, and Development," or WHD.[4] WHD is a concept developed by WHO which aims to benefit women's health and enhance women's role and participation in health by establishing a framework and elements for program development. The health of a family, community, or nation, WHD asserts, cannot be achieved without ensuring the health of women (and mothers).

WORLD HEALTH ORGANIZATION RESOLUTIONS ON WHD

WHD in the European Region of the World Health Organization (EURO), in which the country of Armenia is located, took Nairobi and the WHA Resolutions seriously. The agents of change pushed and saw to it that a *Regional* resolution on WHD was passed in 1989. The Focal Point for WHD in EURO reviewed every single program in EURO for its inclusion or exclusion of WHD and made recommendations, based on Nairobi, for change.[5]

---

[3]Ibid.

[4]Report of the World Conference to Review and Appraise the Achievements of the United Nations Decade for Women: Equality, Development, and Peace (1985). Also, M. Farrell and M. Higgs, "AIDS Prevention: Overcoming Gender Barriers." Paper presented at Conference of the Women and AIDS Prevention Project (Chicago: University of Illinois, July 25, 1994).

[5]M. Farrell and C. Kiaer, "Survey of European Regional Office Professional Staff on Women, Health, and Development," (Copenhagen: European Regional Office, World Health Organization, 1988), and "Plan of Action on Women, Health, and Development in the European Regional Office." (Copenhagen: European Regional Office, World Health Organization, 1987).

THE VIENNA STATEMENT

As a result, the Vienna Statement was written. This latest document (1994) reflects the issues and concerns of women from Central and Eastern Europe, and focuses on six priority areas for action. These include:

- reduced maternal death and increased maternal safety;
- promotion of sexual and reproductive health;
- the introduction of woman-friendly reimbursement policies;
- promotion of programs for healthy lifestyles;
- reducing violence against women; and,
- improving the situation of women working in the health care system.[6]

RATIONALE FOR GLOBAL INITIATIVES FOR WHD

Clearly the policy basis and public health agenda for WHD have been well-established, both globally and regionally. The elements of programs have been developed, and governments and international organizations have acknowledged the necessity for action. But what are the basic underlying factors specific to women? Are the differences between men and women enough to warrant a 1992 World Health Assembly assertion that "women's health must be given the highest level of visibility and urgency?" Is there any physical basis to these assertions? What does the research on the growth and development of women and men over the life span tell us about the gender differences between the two? Women overall live longer than men and have lower mortality rates at all ages and for all causes of death. But are death rates the only indicators needed to assess the differences?

---

[6]Vienna statement on investing in women's health in the countries of Central and Eastern Europe. Copenhagen: European Regional Office for Europe, February 1994.

Gender Differences in Human Growth and Variation

Gender differences play a major role in growth, development, and survival from fertilization onward. Studies of human embryos indicate that a greater number of male fetuses are lost (miscarriages, stillbirths), indicating more susceptibility to disease, poor nutrition, or hypozia. The bones of the female fetus ossify in advance of the male; by seven months a marked priority of the female is well documented and females reach a given stage of maturation at an earlier age. Among different-gender twins who have the same gestational age, the female twin is more advanced in maturation at birth while the male newborn is longer and heavier

Progressive Differences Throughout Childhood

These differences become progressively greater in childhood. Their growth is better canalized with less deviations from genetically established patterns throughout childhood. Growth of males is more affected by adverse environmental insults. In the Longitudinal Studies of Child Health and Development conducted by the Department of Maternal and Child Health of the Harvard School of Public Health,[7] pregnant women were studied in their health, nutrition, and lifestyle; their newborns were evaluated at birth and followed periodically every three months to two years, every six months to 10, yearly to 18, and at 20, 30, 40, and 50 years.

The results of the study showed that girls at all ages had a higher number of illness but lower severity rates, girls exhibited a more vigorous catch-up growth period when the insult was corrected, they bounced back; they are more

---

[7]I. Valadian, H.C. Stuart, and R.B. Reed, "Patterns of Illness Experiences," *Pediatrics* 24:5 (Part II, 1959), p. 941.

buffered, more resilient.[8] This characteristic has been validated in numerous studies of the human and other species and has been shown to exist since prehistoric times.[9] In archeological studies of skeletons in England,[10] in the American Southwest,[11] and in other countries, bones generally affected by some infection showed less scarring among women, thus again demonstrating their resilience when compared with men.

In all industrialized countries today, males have a higher mortality than females at all ages, resulting in a life expectancy at birth for women exceeding that of males by six to seven years. More recently life expectations in both sexes have increased in industrialized countries, but are greater for women. For example, Japanese women have a life expectancy at birth which now exceeds 80 years. A widespread hypothesis explains this biological advantage (or termed by some investigators, biological superiority) by the presence of the two X chromosomes of the female which is linked to immuno-regulatory genes for coping with life-threatening illnesses, resulting in high Igm concentrations and formation of antibodies to infectious agents.[12]

However in a number of countries, particularly the less

---

[8]Ibid.

[9]L.W. Konisberg and W.E. Grant, "Females Better Buffered? Past and Ethnographic Present," *American Journal of Physical Anthropology* (Supplement 18, 1994), p. 124.

[10]C.A. Roberts and B. Margerison, "Male and Female Susceptibility to Infectious Diseases: A Study of British Skeletal Population and Historical Records," *American Journal of Physical Anthropology* (Supplement 18, 1994), p. 170.

[11]Konisberg and Grant, "Females Better Buffered?"

[12]P.L. Stuart-Macadam, "Female Biological Superiority: An Overview," *American Journal of Physical Anthropology* (Supplement 18, 1994), p. 191.

developed, underprivileged ones, this biological advantage disappears, and life expectancies of the female at best equal that of the males, but more often lag behind. Such statistics are a red flag, pointing to chronic malnutrition, poor general health, and poor care of the female.

SOCIAL FACTORS

Socially underprivileged humans display poor growth and health. In addition, in many countries cultural practices give preference to male children; little girls and women are the last to be fed where resources are scarce, they are taken to receive health care only when very sick, and receive less preventive care. Smaller numbers of girls are immunized. Sons are perceived as an economic asset to the family contributing productive labor; daughters are seen as a burden, who should be provided a dowry, whose economic productivity will benefit the husband's family. As a result, the health of women is subordinated to usually male-oriented social dictates.

AIDS IN WOMEN: AN EXAMPLE

The AIDS epidemic is another incidence which at once demonstrates the physiological resilience of women, the adverse effects on women's health of their social and economic disenfranchisement, and the urgent need for women to act as agents of change. Men not women have until now been considered biologically the more vulnerable sex with a death illness record exceeding that of women. Yet in the Americas, Western Europe, and sub-Saharan Africa, AIDS is the leading cause of death for women 20-40 years old,[13] and women constitute the fastest growing category of sufferers in the

---

[13]Centers for Disease Control, "Women and AIDS: The Growing Crisis," *HIV/AIDS Prevention* 2:1 (1991), pp. 1-20.

epidemic.[14] An array of factors may account for this discrepancy, including delayed diagnosis, inferior access to health care, poor use of services, and physiological factors such as the immaturity of the genital tract, vulnerability to tissue trauma, and immature development of vaginal secretions. Thus, while men are considered more vulnerable, women with AIDS do not survive as long after diagnosis as men, and once diagnosed, they become sick faster and die sooner than men with AIDS in spite of their resiliency.[15] Sex-specific socio-economic, and physiological indicators would certainly help in distinguishing the gender differences.

In Canada, HIV positive women are asking for research on women.[16] They are seeking answers to questions such as: How do the antiretroviral drugs work in women's bodies? What treatments are particularly helpful for women? How does this disease affect womens' bodies?

In general, because research protocols insist that women be free of pregnancy and that they do not use contraception, many women are eliminated from research efforts. Consequently, researchers have discouraged female subjects from enrolling, and women have been unable to access treatment protocols. Thus, sex-specific indicators on women are less available than they are for men.

ENVIRONMENTAL FACTORS

These health-related gender differentials are determined by a complex of biological, social, economic, and cultural

---

[14]J. Mann, D. Tarantola, and T. Netter, (eds.). *AIDS in the World* (Cambridge, MA: Harvard University Press, 1992), p. 9.

[15]S. Smeltzer and B. Whipple "Women and HIV Infection, *Image*, 23 (1991), pp. 249-56.

[16]C. Johnston, "Many Canadians Unaware of AIDS' Impact on Women," *Journal of the Canadian Medical Association* 150:2 (1994), pp. 247-49.

factors interacting with genetic endowment;[17] where environment is poor, genetic influence is minimized, and environment overrides. Environment consists of a wide range of factors including altitude, climate, water and air pollution, infection, and radiation. Often two or more combine and result in a greater effect than from one factor operating alone. For example, birth weights tend to be low in high altitude.[18] In addition, hypertension is a frequent complication of pregnancy[19] especially among those recently moving to high altitude areas. Thus, newcomers will not have experienced the lifelong adaptation of those born in the area.[20]

Smoking also results in low birth weight.[21] When a

---

[17]N. Cameron, "The Interaction of Heredity and Environment in the Control of Human Growth and Development," *American Journal of Physical Anthropology*, (Supplement 18, 1994), p. 64.

[18]J.A. Lichty, Y.T. Rosalin, P.D. Burns, and F. Dyar, "Studies of Babies Born at High Altitude: (1) Relation of Altitude to Birth Weight," and (2) R.C. Hofward, J.A. Lichty, and P.D. Burns, "Measurement of Birth Weight, Body Length, and Head Size," *AMA Journal of Diseases of Children* 93 (1957), p. 666, 670.

[19]S.K. Palmer, et al., "Altitude and Hypertensive Complications of Pregnancy," *American Journal of Physical Anthropology* (Supplement 18, 1994), p. 158.

[20]A.R. Frisancho, et al., "Influence of Developmental Acclimation and Activity Level in Bioenergetic Adaptation to High Altitude Hypoxia," *American Journal of Physical Anthropology* (Supplement 18, 1994), p. 89.

[21]D. Rush, "Maternal Smoking: A Reassessment of the Association with Perinatal Mortality," *American Journal of Epidemiology* 96 (1972), p. 183; and J.L. Lyon et al., "Smoking and Carcinoma in situ of the Uterine Cervix," *American Journal of Public Health* 73: 5 (1983A), p. 558; and G. Oster, T.E. Delea and G.A. Colditz, "Maternal Smoking During Pregnancy and Expenditures of Neonatal Health Care," *American Journal of Preventive Medicine* 4:4 (1988), p. 216.

woman moves to a high altitude community, and if she smokes, the result is aggravated further. In addition, in many high altitude areas, people are poor and infectious diseases widespread. The outcome of these combinations is disastrous.

Harmful chemicals (over 50,000 to 75,000 are known) include for example lead,[22] insecticides, and PCB.[23] And over 1,000 new chemicals are discovered each year found in food, human milk, water, air, clothes, homes, and workplaces. Radiation from nuclear power plants, mining of uranium, wastes from nuclear reactors, as well as diagnostic and therapeutic use of radiation have harmful cumulative, long-term effects.[24] "Long-term" refers to effects experienced over

---

[22]J.S. Lin Fu, "Vulnerability of Children to Lead Exposure and Toxicity," *New England Journal of Medicine* 289 (1973), p. 1229.

[23]H.J. Miller et al., "Organochloride Insecticides and Polychlorinated Biphlyl in Human Milk," in W.B. Deichmann, *Toxicology and Occupational Medicine* (New York: Elsevier, 1978), p. 379.

[24]Report of the Advisory Committee on the Biological Effects of Ionizing Radiation: The Effect on Populations of Exposure to Low Levels of Ionizing Radiation (National Academy of Science-National Research Council, 1972). See also M.B. Meyer and J. Tonascia, "Long-term Effects of Prenatal X-Ray of Human Females," *American Journal of Epidemiology* 114:3 (1981), p. 327; A.M. DeKaban, "Abnormalities in Children Exposed to X-Irridiation During Various Stages of Gestation," *Journal of Nuclear Medicine* 22 (1968), p. 322; D. Hoffman, R. Felten, and W.H. Cyr, "Effects of Ionizing Radiation on the Developing Embryo and Fetus: A Review." (Geneva: Bureau of Radiological Health, World Health Organization, 1981); G. Plummer, "Anomalies Occuring in Children Exposed in Utero to the Atomic Bomb in Hiroshima," *Pediatrics* 10 (1952), p. 687; and D. Grahn and J. Dratchman, "Variation in Neonatal Death Rate and Birth Weight in the United States and Possible Relations to Environmental Radiation, Geology, and Altitude," *American Journal of Human Genetics* 15 (1963), p. 329.

the life span. For example, if the fetus is exposed to radiation, the newborn may be stillborn or have malformations. However, some malformations may appear later in childhood, such as poor growth, cancer, or leukemia. Adult women, when exposed, may also experience cancer, such as cancer in situ of the cervix.

DEMOGRAPHICS

Increases in life expectancy and the decline in birth rates have resulted in a general aging of the global populations. Women account for much larger proportions of people over 65 years of age in most CCEE/NIS countries, with the proportion of elderly females almost double of that of males.[25] These women tend to live alone; they live poorly, without family and other means of social support, and may experience poor health. For example, they are postmenopausal and have lost the protection of estrogen against cardiovascular diseases or osteoporosis.

With the changing structures and living situations, women are caring for larger families, often under more disadvantaged conditions. In families with women as head of the household, poverty tends to be the rule. To add to the burden, women remain less educated than men, many having attended only primary school. In the countries of Central and Eastern Europe, the income of women is only about 70 percent of the income of men. The work they do is characterized as burdensome, and it is estimated that women "perform 44 percent of the dangerous work and more than their share

---

[25]Highlights on Women's Health in CCEE and NIS. (Copenhagen: European Regional Office, World Health Organization, February 1994).

of night shift."[26]

Governments often assume that, because women provide the bulk of care in the home, their efforts cost nothing and are of no economic value. In a comprehensive study by Ward and Brown (1992), the "kin work" provided by American women in caring for a family member with AIDS amounted to 8.5 hours per day. The cost, if calculated at a rate of $5.15 per hour, comes to $15,997.88 per year. If housework is added at the reported level of 19 hours per week, an annual value of unpaid care to a person with AIDS is $25,857. Researchers have also found that women performed significantly more hours of housework than men (19.1 and 9.8 respectively).[27]

In the countries of Eastern Europe and the Newly Independent States (NIS), women carry far greater burdens of work in the home yet have the same official working hours as men plus responsibility for running households and caring for the family. In one country, it was found that 42 percent of the men take no part in family life, and they rarely share maternity leave benefits.[28] Women, then, face the double burden of official and kin work.

THE ADDED INFLUENCES OF WORLD EVENTS

The everyday life of women will continue to challenge agents of change. Added to the work of children, the home, and the workplace, additional strains continue to be felt from war, migration, and natural and man-made disasters.

---

[26]J. Shapiro, "The Industrial Labour Force," *Perestroika and Soviet Women*, M. Buckley, ed. (Cambridge: Cambridge University Press, 1992).

[27]D. Ward and M.A. Brown, "Labor and Cost in AIDS Family Caregiving," *Western Journal of Nursing Research* 16:1 (1994), pp. 10-25.

[28]Highlights on women's health in CCEE and NIS.

Families have moved to urban areas and massive migrations have occurred in several parts of the world. These events have brought with them large refugee populations, often of women left behind with children while husbands seek employment.

Just recently, in one part of Eastern Europe and in Haiti, stories emerged as single isolated incidents. Now the world has learned of the full horror of excessive nationalism expressed in the most gruesome fashion as women are raped as part of the planned war offensive by all parties in the conflicts. No numbers on the incidence of HIV are available, but money is reportedly spent on weapons and emergency treatment. After these atrocities were made public in the spring of 1994, a BBC commentator took issue with a Danish physician for making too much of the practice, for after all, he noted, rape has always been part and parcel of war for centuries. So now HIV and AIDS will constitute one more unfortunate reality to add to womens' lives during war time.[29]

CONCLUSIONS AND RECOMMENDATIONS

While much progress has been made, much remains to be done. The governments of the world, the United Nations, including WHO, have taken measures to focus on the issues and needs of women. But much more is needed urgently.

Armed with an understanding of the biological determinants of women, and with a sensitivity to those instances when these boundaries are violated, women as agents of change can work to improve the situation for the world's women in their own countries, and in their own neighborhoods.

---

[29]Farrell and Higgs, "AIDS Prevention: Overcoming Gender Barriers."

What can be done? National and international groups, such as the Armenian International Women's Association, can contact WHO and other organizations and develop the following elements, structures, and processes.

ELEMENTS

Women agents of change can:

• support research which further analyzes the growth and development throughout the life span;

• support the development of targeted, focused, projects on women's health giving priority to issues having the most serious effects on women's health and development;

• support fellowships, grants, educational opportunities, and exchange programs to train women, according to their own interests and abilities; and,

• support projects which enable men to develop, earn a living, and learn about their own health through materials which by their very nature also promote women and children's health and development.

STRUCTURE

Women agents of change can:

• establish offices for women's health in each country;

• establish linkages with organizations of similar interests in order to avoid duplication and to maximize effects.

PROCESSES

Women agents of change can:

• develop reliable information data bases on WHD;

• conduct regular, periodic, national, regional, and international meetings on WHD;

• communicate the information available on WHD to international and private organizations, governmental organizations, to the media, and to the public; and,

• provide public recognition and support for women who are able to listen, respond, and serve the world's women.

Women's groups can also work to further develop local, regional, national, and international policies that support women's development and promote their health. They can insist that every grant funded include prevention guidelines for HIV in the workplace and that no grant be funded without them. Precautions required at all levels must be in place to protect workers uninitiated in the dangers of contaminants in the workplace. The WHO guidelines for counselling and testing must also be included as part of projects, supplies and equipment, and procedures.[30]

Finally, but of equal importance, the role of *men* must be underscored as they, in many places possess the power, authority, control over men-women relationships (tribal or gang), and family and community resources, including the political process and the media.

THE WAY FORWARD

In conclusion, one must observe that all these resources represent potentially enormous opportunities, should they be harnessed to promote the development of the world's most valuable resource—its women. With a sound, scientific basis established, and the physical and biological determinants of women's growth and development determined, sensitivity and responsiveness to the factors which threaten those features should prevail. If they do, women can harness these resources and best serve as active agents of change to improve the lives of all women in the world—including their own.

---

[30]M. Farrell (in press), *HVB and HIV: A Practical Guide for the Healthcare Setting* (Geneva: The World Health Organization Global Program on AIDS).

Armenian National Program on Reproductive Health

Mary Khachikian*

ABSTRACT

The current situation in Armenia has been recognized by the Armenian Parliament as an economic and social crisis. Under these conditions it has become difficult to solve existing health problems, and enormous new problems have been created, in particular, in reproductive health. Based on the current family planning and sexual reproductive health situation and on the country's own national policy of population growth, the National Program on Reproductive Health has been developed by the Armenian Ministry of Health together with the Armenian Family Health Association.

The summit goal of the Program is improvement of health of the family as a whole, including both spouses and their children. The several key programmatic issues that need to be addressed to improve family planning and sexual reproductive health services in Armenia have been identified. They include:

1. The lack of sexual and contraceptive education and limited experience of providers with education and counselling of family planning users.

*Mary Khachikian, M.D., is Chief Specialist on Human Reproduction for the Ministry of Health in Armenia and President of the Armenian Family Health Association.

2. The lack of collection and monitoring of national statistical data required for decision-making by the health authorities.

3. Limited family health services available and limited capacity of health authorities to plan, manage, and sustain such services.

4. Chronic shortages in contraceptive supplies and medications required for the treatment of sexually transmitted diseases, infertility, and miscarriage.

5. Limited options of modern and effective methods of fertility regulation.

6. Over-reliance on induced abortion as a method of birth control. Limited options of modern and safe methods of pregnancy termination.

7. Limited experience of (para)medical professionals with diagnosis and management of sexually transmitted diseases.

8. Deficiencies of sexual and reproductive health education of adolescents and youth, and limited services for their counselling.

9. The absence of an effective system for the referral of patients with diseases or disorders in sexual reproductive health.

10. The lack in the antenatal counselling service and perinatal care of pregnant women.

11. The high level of environmental air pollution and other hazards with possible adverse impact on human reproduction.

DISCUSSION

We think Mary has an illustration of the strength of Armenian women relative to abortion from Armenia. Mary gives us an example of women's resiliency as it applies to Armenia.

SITUATION OF INDUCED ABORTION IN YEREVAN

SURVEY OF 4,349 MARRIED WOMEN, AGED 15-44 YEARS

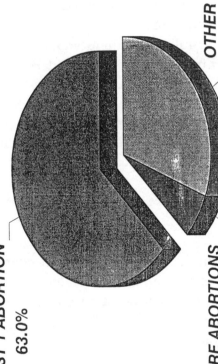

AT LEAST 1 ABORTION
63.0%

OTHER
30.7%

10 OR MORE ABORTIONS
6.3%
5% OF THEM - COMPLICATIONS
AFTER LAST ABORTION

FIGURE 1   SOURCE: M. KHACHIKIAN, 1991

I should say that all couples and individuals in Armenia have the right to decide freely the number and spacing of their children. Since 1955, by the regulation of the former Soviet government, abortion is legal. Before twelve weeks of gestation it is permitted on request, but afterwards only for medical or certain social reasons.

However illegal abortions performed out of the hospital are not the exception, and they result in some cases in women's deaths.

When the fifteen Republics of the former Soviet Union are compared on the basis of the abortion rate, Armenia takes one of the last places. However this data is underestimated because of certain social reasons, such as out-of-pocket payment. Not all cases of induced abortion are being registered at the hospital. For many gynecologists pregnancy termination is the main way to earn money.

To evaluate the real reproductive health situation in Armenia in 1990-1992, a survey was conducted of over 4,000 currently married Armenian women of reproductive age. It was conducted in Yerevan in collaboration with the World Health Organization. The results of this study indicated that induced abortion is still the main method of fertility regulation. You may see nearly 63 percent (Fig. 1) of currently married women in Armenia had at least one induced abortion and 6.3 percent had ten or more abortions. I think this is a very high rate.

Our study reveals also that the limited family planning services available, the lack of contraception education, and the shortage of contraceptives were the main reasons for such behavior.

The next slide presents the contraceptive use pattern in Armenia which will help you understand the situation, (see Fig. 2). The total contraceptive prevalence in the survey population was 56 percent; however the combined percentage of women using no contraceptives or depending on the less

CONTRACEPTIVE PREVALENCE AND USE PATTERN IN YEREVAN

SURVEY OF 4,349 MARRIED WOMEN, AGED 15-44 YEARS

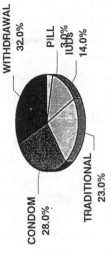

WITHDRAWAL
32.0%

PILL
3.0%

IUD'S
14.0%

TRADITIONAL
23.0%

CONDOM
28.0%

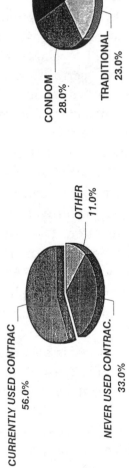

OTHER
11.0%

CURRENTLY USED CONTRAC
56.0%

NEVER USED CONTRAC.
33.0%

FIGURE 2   **SOURCE: M. KHACHIKIAN, 1991**

reliable methods was extremely high when compared to Western European countries. The most popular means of fertility regulation were withdrawal and barrier methods. The hormonal contraceptive pills have been rarely used—only 3 percent. The I.U.D. was twice less popular than the barrier methods. Other modern methods such as sterilization, injectional implants, etc., have been unknown. That summarizes the abortion and contraceptive situation.

Mary attended the Cairo Conference and would like to tell us about it...

The International Conference on Population and Development was held in Cairo in May 1994. There were about 4,000 participants from all over the world. The forum of non-governmental organizations was held parallel with the main conference. Every country presented its own experiences and statements on population and developmental issues. The Armenian delegation submitted the national report, which was recognized as one of the best reports among the former Soviet republics.

In addressing the mandate of the International Conference on Population and Development, its overall theme on population, sustained economic growth, and sustained development, the participants were guided by the following principles:

Principle 1. Everyone is entitled to all the rights and freedoms set forth in the Universal Declaration of Human Rights, without distinction of any kind such as race, color, sex, language, religion, political or other opinion, national or social origin, property, birth, or other status.

Principle 2. People are the most important and valuable resources that a nation possesses. A country should ensure that all individuals are given the opportunity to make the most of their potential. People have the right to an adequate standard of living for themselves and their families, including adequate food, clothing, and housing.

Principle 3. Advancing gender equality and empowerment of woman is a constant of population and development-related programs. Men and women have the same equal right to participate in policy and decision-making at all levels.

Extract from Principle 6. The international conference on population and development reaffirms the need for the full integration of the countries with economies in transition as well as all other countries into the world economy.

Principle 7. Everyone has the right to liberty and security of person and the right to the enjoyment of the highest attainable standard of physical and mental health. The state should take all appropriate measures to ensure on the basis of the equality of men and women universal access to health care services, including these related to sexual and reproductive health care and family planning.

Individuals have the basic right to decide fully and responsibly the number and spacing of their children and to have the information, education, and means to do so.

During the years between 1960 and 1980, with the improvement of health and living standards in Armenia, the mortality rate decreased and average life expectancy for both sexes increased from 69 years in 1958 to 72.6 years in 1980. But the figures remain at approximately the same level in the following years.

The comparison of the life expectancy in different countries and regions of the world indicated that in 1988 the life expectancy in Armenia was seven years longer compared to demographically developing groups of countries, but still five years shorter than an average for the formerly Soviet Union and established market economies.

On the average women in Armenia as in most of the countries live longer than men. Thus a newborn girl born in Armenia in 1992 can expect to live about 76 years, or nine years longer than a newborn boy. Furthermore women have lower mortality rates for all causes of death at all ages.

When looking at these indicators, the impression is often given that women are healthier than men. However, it is a erroneous conclusion since a few years differential in the average survival time had higher chronic illnesses and disability associated with longer survival which is the biological advantage of woman as was explained to us.

Among the causes of women's death in Armenia, maternal mortality is important since it is mainly preventable. I want to show you (Fig. 3).

In the years 1987 to 1989 the average maternal mortality in Armenia was 40. And in the following three years, 1990 to 1992, it has dropped to 38.5. However this indicator is still higher than the WHO target for Europe of no more than 15 maternal deaths per 100,000 live births, and considerably higher than the European community average of 8.8 per 100,000 live births.

The main causes of maternal death in Armenia are hemorrhage, gestation hypertension, abortion, abortion complications, and infection. I think that most of these causes are preventable.

We have found that the health of women is often subordinate to usually male-oriented social dictates. Mary, what about in Armenia?

I should say that traditionally in Armenia children are the most important component of the family, and the failure to have children is often a cause for divorce. On the average there are two children in an Armenian family. The main

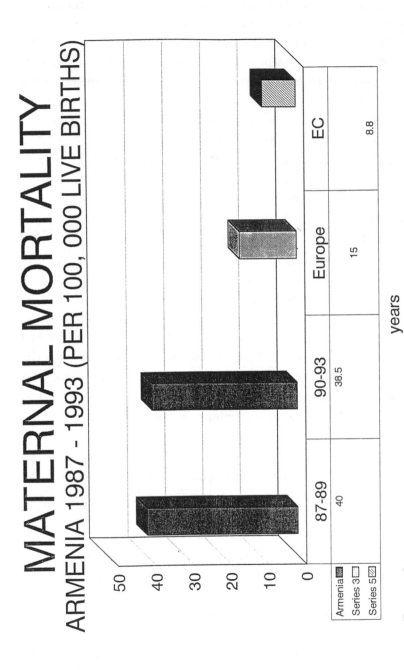

FIGURE 3

Source: 1.Ministry of Health, 2. Stephenson & Wagner

reason for having a third or the following child is wishing to have the desired number of boys and girls. The cultural practice is to give preference to male children; however, after their birth, daughters usually receive similar attention and love from their parents.

We spoke about the health problems arising from pollutants in the environment. Can you comment about the situation in Armenia?

Yes, you are right, and I want to add that our altitude due to its geographical location and the concentration of industry and transport in the city of Yerevan results in high levels of pollution. The more precise ecological situation in Armenia you will learn from other presentations. I would like to concentrate on the new environmental factors which face Armenia today. The long term economic blockade by neighboring countries, the deterioration of the economy after the collapse of the ex-Soviet Union, the undeclared war over Nagorno-Karabagh, and the severe earthquake of 1988 have led to an acute shortage of food, energy, petrol, and medical supplies. The new problems are being created with housing, feeding, watering, heating of houses, and sanitation. The long-term psychological stress, the cold in winter, malnutrition, and lack of sanitation are the new environmental factors facing the Armenian population.

Certain groups of the population have been more adversely affected than others, and these require more assistance than others. Among them are refugees, displaced persons, and earthquake victims. Others considered at risk are children under five, pregnant women, mothers, and elderly people.

Because of the blockade, Armenians are now depending almost entirely on their own resourcefulness and on foreign humanitarian aid which helps us to survive in these circumstances. And taking this opportunity, on behalf of the

Armenian people, I would like to express my sincere gratitude to all of you in the diaspora who shared with us in our difficulties.

CONCLUSION

I would like to thank Marie Farrell and Isabelle Valadian for their conclusions and recommendations which are directed to the health of all women including those in Armenia. I just want to add a statement which probably applies to all countries with economies in transition.

There is a strong relationship between women's health, environment, and economic development of the society. The achievement of sustainable development has become a necessity for Armenia as well as for all other countries with economies in transition. International cooperation to create conditions for sustainable development on global levels is required. In the areas of national and international conflicts, governments and women's organizations should take necessary measures in efforts for peace.

Second, there is an urgent need to strengthen the reproductive health care and family planning service provision in Armenia as in other countries with economies in transition. Reproductive health and family planning are human rights, and family health benefit programs, whether governmental, non-governmental, or private, should be supported.

Third, there is a global need for increasing international cooperation in regard to environmental protection. Every country including Armenia should make efforts to prevent environmental degradation. Those countries who are in extreme situations should receive assistance from the international community.

Woman and the Environment

Gariné Danielian*

In all of the important international conventions, beginning with the Declaration of the United Nations Conference in Rio de Janeiro and "The Agenda for the 21st Century," a great role is attributed to woman's participation in the decision-making process for problems of an ecological nature and, more broadly, in the development and propagation of ecological ethics. The role of women is also central in providing the younger generation with an ecologically sensitive education and upbringing.

As a result of the Karabagh conflict and the blockade, the ecological situation in Armenia has deteriorated. In the past four years the water reserves of Lake Sevan have been used once again for the purposes of hydroelectric energy. As a result, the level of water in the lake has been lowered by almost one meter [3.2 feet]. In the Republic 1.5 million trees have been cut down and used for heating (in place of which some 2 million trees have been planted, with significant assistance from the diaspora). Because of the energy crisis, the purifying stations of the sewers have not functioned to the full extent, thus increasing the pollution of the rivers Hrazdan, Vorotan, Akhurian, Voghji, and others with certain elements.

Gariné Danielian is senior scientist at Yerevan State University and the former Minister of Environmental Affairs for the Republic of Armenia.

The fact that the government is unable to allot means for anti-storm and anti-mud-flow measures causes the utmost danger. It is important to constantly conduct this kind of work in Armenia, otherwise we might regularly face natural disasters. A vivid example of such a situation occurred in May 1994, when an accident took place at one of two water-tanks of Artik (Vardaghbyur), and only the fact that the second tank was able to withhold the enormous flow of water prevented the nearby villages from a tragedy.

Hence there can be only one answer to the question of how women of the diaspora can help to improve the ecological situation in Armenia: by fighting against the blockade.

And the entire diaspora, especially the women, are helping a great deal. And to confront the second problem—to put into practice ecological thinking and education in Armenia—we need literature, professionally prepared films, and other information that women of the diaspora can help to provide for us.

(Translated by Anahit Tovmassian Shahinian)

Protection of the Environment: Politics and Law

Aida Iskoyan*

Protection of the environment is one of the most global problems concerning all mankind, regardless of social-political structure or degree of economic development. Environmental protection affects the lives of both women and men, but the former, by nature and essence, perceive the ecological problems influencing life and prosperity more acutely and delicately.

It is evident that recognition and solution of the environmental protection problem depends on the social-economic situation. The present difficult economic and social-political situation on Armenia has aggravated already strained and unfavorably ecological conditions.

The problem of environmental protection has exploded into the social-political life of the Republic along with the Karabagh spring of 1988. Since that time it has not lost its urgency, and has acquired some new, unforeseen features.

The known events in the region, namely closing of the atomic energy station, the blockade of the railway, and continued explosions of the gas pipeline, have become the causes of the acute energy crisis in the Republic. The result of these processes is degradation of the environment. Against this background emerges again and again the problem of environmental protection and rational exploita-

*Aida Iskoyan is professor of Law at Yerevan State University.

tion of resources.

For Armenia this issue is equivalent to the problem of the nation's survival, which is impossible to solve without the real participation of women, who constitute more than one-half of the population of the Republic of Armenia.

In this situation there appears the clear necessity for new approaches towards working out the national strategy, geopolitics, as well as criteria for the participation of the Republic in international cooperation.

Law ranks high in the system of environmental protection measures. At present there exists legislation in the Republic regulating relationships in the sphere of ecology. But these legal regulations are not always realized in practice.

It is therefore important to analyze the following: (1) the current state of legislation in Armenia in the field of environmental protection; (2) reasons for the low effectiveness of environmental protection legislation; and (3) ways to improve the effectiveness of environmental protection legislation (what must be done to make the mentioned legislation "work better").

Having studied the experience of environmental legislation in action, the author emphasizes the importance of the following: (1) the objective increase of the ecological factor in the life of society; (2) realization of the internal economic essence of ecological problems; (3) equal priority, inner unity, and inward interdependency of the ecological, social, and economic needs of society; and (4) need to choose a strategy of national development under which the ecological-social-economic optimum is reached.

In this connection emerges the role of public participation in environmental protection as one of the factors in ensuring the effectiveness of ecological legislative action.

Analysis of the situation in Armenia in the indicated aspect allows us to acknowledge the insufficient participation of women in the processes occurring in the Republic, namely in environmental protection.

It is of paramount significance to make maximum use of women's interaction between the ecological movement on the one hand, and the bodies of state power and government in the sphere of nature exploitation on the other. It is necessary to envisage measures of a legal nature to support women's non-governmental organizations and associations, including measures of financial state assistance.

It is also proposed to convene periodically an ecological women's forum, where various aspects of environmental protection and the role of women in it would be discussed.

A high level of ecological legislation, in the author's opinion, is undoubtedly of great value for society, for its movement toward a favorable environment, and toward ensuring real equality for women.

The Role of Social Consciousness in the Problems of Environmental Protection

Rita A. Ayvazova*

In the Republic of Armenia, as a result of the interaction of a series of political, economic, and environmental factors, an ecological situation has been created which is unique in the region in its high level of risk.

During the Soviet period the development of large industries in the Republic provided positive solutions to economic problems, but at the same time serious difficulties of anthropogenic pollution in the environment resulted. This pollution in turn aroused the dissatisfaction of the population, which went out into the streets demanding the closing of large enterprises.

The thoughtless actions resulting from the ecological situation brought to a halt the principal enterprises and the nuclear energy station, thus creating industrial disorder and rupturing the close economic ties with the other Soviet Republics, from whom Armenia imported the principal part of its essential products and energy.

The full economic blockade of the Republic of Armenia placed the nation in a position of dying out from cold and hunger. Insufficient consumption of food, especially milk and creamery products, threatened biological harm to human organisms, especially as reflected in the development of the

Rita A. Ayvazova is chief ecologist for the City of Yerevan.

growing generation, the children.

The present physiological level of survival has influenced the consciousness of the nation. On the first plane are questions of securing the basic necessities of life. The serious social situation created conditions leading to the predatory consumption of resources (water, trees, animals).

Measures for protecting nature are not under sufficient government control. In the absence of a comprehensive policy to deal with the complex problems of protecting nature, no scientific approach has been elaborated with concrete recommendations for dealing with the situation.

In the present circumstances more efficient state ecological control, on the basis of newly developed criteria, is essential.

Given the current conditions, most of society is firmly convinced of the necessity of quickly reopening the nuclear power station and restarting the largest enterprises with full power ("Nairit" factory, for example), without taking into consideration the possible consequences.

In this way a unique ecological situation has been created in terms of its high risk, especially taking the geographic situation of Armenia into consideration this in turn is highly dangerous ecologically for the entire region.

For this reason the problem goes beyond the boundaries of the Republic and requires the participation of neighboring and interested countries, as well as the mediation of international organizations, in order to work out and put into effect complex, carefully considered measures to avoid new mistakes.

Most Endangered Species: Children of Armenia

Vartiter Kotcholosian Hovannisian*

Armenia's at-will bankrupt economy locked in by a peculiarly selective perpetual blockade has uprooted the foundations of the nation's civic life and traditional civility. After accounting for the country's brain drain, for a narrow class of the untouched ex-regime's elite, and for the well-insulated class of *nouveaux riches*, there remains at the mercy of the world community the dehumanized, low-profile majority. Hardened by the lessons of a cruel double-standard reality and socio-political duplicity, I shall not dwell on the plight of the forsaken elderly, the ever-deprived women, the stupefied unemployed professionals-artisans-laborers, the sad victims of a wrecked educational system, and not even on the vegetating masses of condemned refugees.

The "bell tolleth" for the most precious and the last natural resource of Armenia—her children. The nation's genetic pool is in jeopardy on the threshold of yet another fierce winter. By now chronically malnourished, some one million children of Armenia and Artsakh will certainly swell the hitherto staggering pediatric and especially perinatal morbidity-mortality statistics. Though no official numbers would be required to confirm the stark reality, statistics

*Vartiter Kotcholosian Hovannisian, M.D., practices internal medicine at the Southern California Permanente Medical Group.

similar to those prepared by our own Centers for Disease Control (CDC) and other US and UN agencies are the absolute prerequisite for any serious intervention.

So much for the gloomy backdrop upon which shine the stellar deeds and accomplishments of several hundred NGOs domestic and foreign non-governmental organizations) and dozens of governmental agencies. It is through the efforts of these dedicated people that Armenia has survived at all the natural and man-made disasters that have occurred since 1988. It is this extraordinary humanitarian effort that still gives hope to the infinitely patient grassroots.

Unfortunate for all, the absence of an effective local coordinating infrastructure and the benefactors' hesitation to implement Western management norms have also resulted in counter-productive inequities and tragic irregularities. As a rule, each and every entity doing its own thing carries its cargo to that one familiar spot and carries back home a halo, feeling rightfully accomplished. There have been numerous aborted efforts to found a central clearinghouse to coordinate all humanitarian deliveries and their distribution. Such a center would facilitate organic continuity to all segments of the population in need. It would also free astronomical overhead monies and trim or eliminate the built-in red-tape expenditures. It must be stated, for the record, that many official agencies or projects spend up to and more than half of the granted funds for their own operational expenses.

In my public appeal, which appeared in the diasporan press last summer, I was urging individuals and organizations to spur the international agencies resident in Armenia to joint, well-coordinated action to save Armenia's children.

The following is a partial list of NGOs and international outposts in Armenia, as derived from interoffice ledgers. Curiously, not included in those lists are some of the most reliable and effective humanitarian relief organizations—

the exemplary Lincy Foundation's United Armenian Fund
(UAF) and intrepid Baroness Caroline Cox's Christian
Solidarity International mission, to name only a few.

*All-Armenian Fund - The President, Republic of Armenia
*American Red Cross
*American University of Armenia
*Armenian Assembly of America
*Armenian General Benevolent Union
*Armenian Missionary Association of America
*Armenian Red Cross
*Armenian Relief Society
*CARE
*Fund for Armenian Recovery
*Fund for Democracy and Development
*Haigazian College
*International Community Association
*International Committee of the Red Cross
*International Executive Service Corps
*International Federation of the Red Cross
*Jewish Distribution Center
*Junior Achievement
*Project HOPE
*Save the Children
*Volunteers in Overseas Cooperative Assistance
*World Rehabilitation Fund P/O Center
*Young Men's Christian Association
*BCEOM
*European Community
*European Community Humanitarian Organization
*United Nations
*UNDP
*United Nations High Commission for Refugees
*UNICEF
*World Bank
*World Bank Project Implementation Unit

*World Food Program
US Agency for International Development
Peace Corps
US Centers for Disease Control
International Organization for Migration
Medicins Sans Frontieres
YMCA Armenia
Medical Outreach for Armenians, Inc., Eastern Region
Aznavour Fund

Those marked with an asterisk are agencies that, in addition to the Health and State Ministries, were urged to action by the USAID Regional Mission (US Agency for International Development). On May 2, 1994, the Mission's director, Suzanne Olds, voiced her concern for the health and well-being of Armenia's children, reinforced by the CDC reports and supported by the US Ambassador to Armenia, Harry S. Gilmore. Updated addresses of the organizations may be obtained from the Armenian Assembly of America in Washington, D.C. or the Yerevan office, which started to serve Armenia immediately after the Dec. 7, 1988 earthquake and recently cut the ribbon for a long-overdue NGO Resource and Training Center.

The challenge to restore Armenia's children to a better future is upon us, individually and collectively.

P.S. Here are examples of unintentional ineffectiveness which compromises every surviving child by stunting his/her physical and intellectual development.

1) The UNICEF office in Armenia works hard in the field of immunization. However, the staff is limited by the WHO's current standards, which cover an arbitrary age range, leaving out the younger and older age groups. Pro-rated amounts of vaccines are made available as projected for under-developed countries and do not include the required

immunizations as accepted for the rest of the world. On the other hand, local health officials' efforts follow the ingrained protocol from the Soviet era, struggling with inadequate supplies of non-standardized vaccines from various unreliable sources. And all involved are waiting for ephemeral new guidelines to revamp the system, while easily preventable and treatable diseases take a high toll among the malnourished subjects.

2) Armenia has no milk of her own for the children. Humanitarian baby-food aid has figured decisively in the survival of this target population. Infant formula and dry milk are delivered in impressive quantities, at times almost implying glut. Yet peaks and valleys of abnormal delivery conditions have created milkless intervals for many children, who are forced to subsist on sweetened water. Also, qualifying age limitations create a crisis when, for instance, the child reaches age two and drops out of the formula list. The transition time to qualify for and obtain a milk-powder subsidy translates into immediate hunger for the toddler. Moreover the milk is often not age-appropriate for these children. The polyclinics distribute powdered milk to the neighborhood preschoolers only sporadically. Older school children do not receive any form of milk. I have been hoping that the Soviet-era cigarette ration coupons, granted at birth to each citizen for life, would be repelled or at least substituted with milk or vitamins, whenever available.

3) Vitamins have been promised by many affected philanthropists visiting the scene, but the follow-through has often been lacking. Medications have been collected and shipped all along, but there has been no professional quality control and no system for effective distribution to date.

Armenian Infant's Nutritional Needs

Seda Khachatrian*

After the collapse of the Soviet Union, the constituent republics lost most of the ties which they had established in the course of many decades. The situation in Armenia deteriorated even further because of the devastating earthquake, blockade lasting for years, the undeclared war in Karabagh, darkness due to the energy shortage, and severe, cold winters following one another. Undoubtedly, because of the simultaneous interaction of these negative factors, the quantity, quality, and variety of the products entering Armenia were drastically reduced. A situation was created which had a negative influence over all age groups of the population, affecting especially children. The number of marriages fell, as did the number of births. Because of the malnutrition of pregnant women, the latter suffered frequently from anemia, the number of birth defects went up, and the number of infants dependent on breast feeding decreased.

The diet of Armenian children consists nowadays mainly of carbohydrates, which even though they increase the body weight, are not healthy, because they do not provide proteins, vitamins, or micro elements, thus producing a negative influence on children's health.

---

*Seda Khachatrian, M.D., is a pediatrician and a department chief at the Third Children's Hospital in Yerevan, Armenia.

Undoubtedly, such a situation leaves its impact on the genetic fund of the nation, and if it were not for the impressive number of unreserved, tireless, faithful, and unselfish pediatricians working everyday to take required measures in the most operative way, the above-mentioned conditions would have caused even more serious results. However, thanks to a series of programs worked out by the Ministry of Health, the condition of our children has recently improved. A great role in this should be attributed to help from abroad, mainly in the form of adapted mixtures and other products which allowed us to rationally organize the diet of the infants at least. Of major importance was also the milk powder received in ample quantity, thus to a certain extent compensating for the deficiency of natural milk.

UNICEF, the Red Cross and Red Crescent, the entire Armenian diaspora, "Aznavour to Armenia," "Armenia Aid Fund," the Eastern Diocese of the Armenian Apostolic Church, and many other organizations and individuals played an active role in this. I would like to particularly mention the organization "Care," which works on a long-term basis to provide help for children and to be faithful to its title. The project becomes especially valuable when one takes into consideration the fact that, thanks to its activities, the children will be receiving milk for a considerable length of time, thus growing up well-developed, coordinated, and healthy.

The representatives of "Care" cooperate mainly with the polyclinics which distribute food and milk among breast-feeding mothers and children personally. The pregnant women get their portion during their gynecological consultations.

I know that you are very eager to learn about your aid getting to the children. Because I participate personally in the distribution, I would like to assure you that each child gets the amount meant for his or her age. Using this opportunity I would like to draw to your attention the letter of the mother of several children, Karine Khachatrian:

> When I had my triplet daughters, I had a mixture of feelings. On one hand, I was rejoicing, but on the other hand I was deeply concerned about what and how I was going to provide them with food, because the family which consisted prior to their birth of seven members was going through very harsh times. To top it all, my husband had lost his job recently. In this desperate situation I was immensely helped by my polyclinic which, with the essential assistance of "Care," was able to supply my three newborns with the necessary amount of food, thanks to which they are growing healthy. I am sending my heartfelt thanks to these people of good will who are helping us out in this dramatic situation.

Providing the children with adapted mixtures is very important and positive, but it is evident that even though they are wholesome in their chemical compositions, these mixtures are devoid of the biological value of maternal milk. Therefore our pediatric services are widely supporting the project "Breast feeding," which is designed for the entire country and has already yielded very positive results.

The pediatricians and nurses of our country, who work under unheard-of, harsh conditions, receiving symbolic low salaries, do everything they can for maintaining the health of our children.

A healthy child means happiness for the family, but for this happiness one must live in peace. That is why our women want peace more than anything else for their children, so that in no corner of the world will there be wars, so that no child is killed by a bullet, so that there is sun and bright sky above our children's heads. Dear friends, let us do everything for peace to rule the Armenian world, and the entire world.

Women's Non-Governmental Organizations (NGOs) in Armenia

Compiled by Gariné Danielian

The following thirteen organizations have participated in this report:
1. Women's Republican Council of Armenia (Established in 1989/1991)
2. Armenian Women's Treaty (1989/1991)
3. Armenia Mother's Fund (1989/1992)
4. Armenian Intellectual Woman (1990/1991)
5. Armenian Woman (1990/1991)
6. Soldier's Mothers Republican Committee (1990/1991)
7. Women's Peace Congress (1990/1992)
8. Armenian Relief Cross (1991)
9. Family Relief Society (1992)
10. Women of Armenian World (1993/1994)
11. Anahid (1993)
12. Khevont Alishan (1993)
13. Pan-Armenian Women's Organization (1994)

The above organizations started taking form during the liberation struggle of Armenia between the years 1985 to 1988. In 1988 the women's movement helped noticeably to advance the democratization efforts in Armenia.

The main thrust and goal of those organizations are to fight for women's rights, to aid in the solution of national problems, and to encourage the establishment of human rights for all.

A few comments about women's conditions in the country:

During the Soviet regime special attention was given to the rights of women—such as equal education, medical care, political election rights, work, and compensation. But since the establishment of the new democratic republic, women's rights have been overlooked. In a parliament of 260 members only 3 percent are women, while in the city council of Yerevan women make up only 10 percent.

In spite of the existing problems in the country and the inequalities that prevail, the woman today is physically and spiritually responsible for the welfare of the family and the children.

A short outline of the work of each organization follows:

1. *Women's Republic Council of Armenia (WRCA)*

The goals of this organization are to represent the rights and welfare of Armenian women to the legislative bodies; to develop laws protecting women, mothers, and children; to create equal rights for women in the election of governmental representatives; to develop laws barring discrimination against women; to develop laws for ownership by women; and to improve the socio-economic conditions of women.

The WRCA has urged local political parties to include the status of women on their agenda and to give special attention to women candidates at the next election.

It is one of the first three organizations to publish a women's weekly and it has established a school with a "twenty-first century leadership program," which is designed to prepare a new generation of national and international leaders.

2. *Armenian Women's Treaty*

This organization has assisted with social events for the

elderly, orphans, children, and wounded soldiers. It has organized classes for orphans, for those who have only one parent, and for the needy. It has supplied medicine and food supplies, especially to the Karabagh inhabitants.

Along with the Solider's Mothers Republican Committee, it has participated in conferences in Moscow where for the first time the Karabagh issue has been discussed.

3. Armenia Mother's Fund

The major purpose of this organization is to assist women in their political and economic endeavors.

It has helped families who have faced economic and social hardships starting sometimes from their pregnancy until their children reach maturity. In the past two years it has helped many families in Yerevan and Gumri. At present it assists 4,312 women who have children aged 3 to 16.

4. Armenian Intellectual Woman's Association

This organization seeks to elevate the women's role in the fields of science, art, and culture by planning lectures and seminars with local and diasporan organizations, thus elevating the status of women. In 1992 it assisted in the establishment of the Armenia Fund.

5. Armenian Woman

The rights of women educators are the focus of the organization. It has been successful in raising the salaries of teachers with establishment of a strike committee. It also has organized four conferences on the role of women in the past and present, and on the Armenian woman as the backbone of the nation.

6. Soldiers' Mothers Republican Committee

This organization was created in order to assist soldiers who were involved in the liberation struggle. It participated in an international conference in 1992 and organized a three-month vacation in Iran for some of the needy children, placing them with Armenian families there.

The Committee has met with the fighting soldiers in Karabagh and delivered their letters to their mothers. It has joined forces with the Armenian Women Treaty and helped the wounded soldiers and the orphans by organizing concerts and exhibits.

7. Women's Peace Congress

The main goal of the organization is to encourage women's participation in the political and social life in the community. It has assisted women who have suffered abuse and discrimination by organizing "Rest Homes" for the women.

8. Armenian Relief Cross

The charitable work of this organization consists of helping needy children. It has constructed four villages as well as some schools and hospitals. It has supplied medicine and clothing to many orphans and needy families. It has participated in offering scholarships to students.

9. Family Relief Society

This organization works to strengthen families, especially by educating the youth. It studies the status of the family in the country and present its findings to the government and organizes seminars and conferences by inviting experts to lecture on family issues.

10. Women of Armenian World

The goal of this organization is to protect the rights of women. It assists mothers of soldiers with health and social issues.

11. *Anahid*

This is a chapter of the organization in England which has developed cultural and charitable programs to help needy families. It assists artist by helping them organize art exhibits in the diaspora.

12. *Khevont Alishan*

The goal of this group is to organize Armenian language and cultural courses for those in need, without requiring financial compensation. Special attention is given to Armenian teachers, mostly women, by trying to elevate their status.

13. *Pan-Armenian Women's Organization*

This newly organized group has the goal of advancing women's role in the political and social arena. It has organized conferences on childbirth and early childhood education and has helped handicapped children by assisting with their schooling. It has also participated in several conferences discussing peace and human rights proposals in Helsinki, Washington, D.C., and other meetings in Armenia and Karabagh.

EPILOGUE

It is important to realize that the non-governmental organizations have not been involved with women's issues only, but they have been active in the life of the nation with all its facets—peace, charity, religious life, national minority rights, and the defense of the principles of democracy.

Women have participated in the liberation of Armenia and the struggle in Karabagh both physically and spiritually. The members of the United Nations have increased from 51 nations to 184 in fifty years due to the liberation and final independence of many nations in Africa and the Middle East. The UN has worked to stabilize new nations through democracy and education. Armenian women also believe that the establishment of democratic ideals and the education of women and children are essential in bringing stability to Armenia, and they hope that their efforts, through the activities of their Non Governmental Organizations, will help the Armenian Republic.

AIWA
ARMENIAN INTERNATIONAL WOMEN'S ASSOCIATION
Armenian Women in a Changing World
PROGRAM

Monday, September 19, 1994

9:00 - 9:45 a.m.
Bishop Partridge Hall

Registration & Coffee

10 a.m. - 11:45
Hoare Memorial Hall

Opening Session
Welcoming Statements
    Agnes K. Missirian, Conference Chair
    Barbara J. Merguerian, AIWA President
Keynote Addresses
Lucia Ter Petrossian, First Lady of Armenia
    "Armenian Women in a Changing World"
Mary Catherine Bateson, Author & Educator
    "Commitment in a Time of Change"

12 noon - 12:45 p.m.
Bishop Partridge Hall

Luncheon

GAINING POWER & INFLUENCE IN GOVERNMENT & BUSINESS

1- 2:45 p.m.
Convocation Hall

Panel Sessions (choose one of three)
<u>Influencing Political Leaders</u>

Emma Aghayan, Former Member, Parliament of Iran
    "Participating in the Political Process in Iran"
Lily Ring Balian, Northrop-Grumman Corp., Los Angeles
    "Participating in the Political Process in the U.S."
Odette Bazil, All-Party Parliamentary Group, London
    "The British Experience"
Hranush Hagopian, Member of Parliament, Armenia
    "The Role of Women in the Political Life of Armenia"
Chair: Gassia Apkarian, Armenian Assembly of America

Room 4

<u>Entrepreneurship and Joint Ventures</u>

Catherine Kessedjian, Attorney, Paris
    "Legal Considerations in Expanding International Trade"
Mariam Nigohosian, AT&T, New York
    "Establishing a Telephone System for Armenia"
Nariné Sahakian, Ministry of the Economy, Armenia
    "The Role of International Organizations"
Kohar Yenokian, Director, Garoon Garment Factories, Armenia
    "The New Economic Climate in Armenia"
Chair: Doris Jafferian, Daniel Webster College

Room 3   Tapping the Power of the Media
                                Salpi Haroutinian Ghazarian, Editor, Armenian International
                                    Magazine, "The Face of Armenians to the World"
                                Joy Renjilian-Burgy, Wellesley College
                                    "Education and the Media"
                                Chair: Natalie Zakarian, Harvard Business School

3:00 - 4:30 p.m.   Workshops (choose one of two)
                                Outreach and Collaborative Programs
                                Rita Balian, Community Activist
                                    "How to Influence Decision-Makers in the U.S. Political Process"
                                Nancy Sweezy, Director, Armenia Cultural Project, Arlington, Mass.
                                    "How to Develop Collaborative Programs"
                                Gulnara Shahinian, Director of Foreign Relations, Yerevan
                                    "Joint Ventures: Some Recent Experiences"
                                Chair: Seta Terzian

Room 3   Career Strategies for Young Professionals
                                Nora Janoyan, Senior Financial Analyst, Paramount Pictures, L.A.

4:30-5:00 p.m.   Afternoon Tea
Bishop Partridge Hall

5:00 - 6:00 p.m.   Presentations (Choose one of two)
                                Images of Armenians

Room 4   Reading by Arlene Voski Avakian, author of Lion Woman's Legacy: An
                                    Armenian-American Memoir
Room 3   Video Presentation by Eva Medzorian, producer of Armenian Women's
                                    Struggle
Convocation Hall   Illustrated Talk by Ruth Thomasian, executive director of Project SAVE

Tuesday, September 20, 1994

7:30 - 8:45 a.m.   Breakfast Discussion for All Participants
                                AIWA's Organization and Expansion

                                THE ARMENIAN HERITAGE: COMMITMENT AND CHANGE
9:00-10:45 a.m.   Panel sessions (choose one of three)
Convocation Hall   Rethinking Armenian Culture: Transmitting the Legacy
                                Erna Shirinian, Library of Ancient Manuscripts, Armenia
                                    "The Image of Armenian Women in History"
                                Ellie Antreassian, AGBU Manoogian-Demirjian School, Los Angeles,
                                    "The Role of Women in Armenian Identity Enhancement in the
                                    Diaspora"
                                Eileen Vartan Barker, London School of Economics
                                    "Critical Issues Facing Armenian Women"

Martiné Hovanessian, University of Strasbourg, France
"Transmitting the Legacy: the Armenian Community In France"
G. Karen Merguerian, Seton Hall University, New Jersey
"Writing Our Own Lives: Armenian Women's Voices in Autobiography"
Chair: Eileen Vartan Barker, London School of Economics

Room 4   Changing Social and Political Roles: A Historical Perspective
Susan Pattie, University of London
"The Armenian Communities of Cyprus and London"
Sona Zeitlian, author, Los Angeles
"Nationalism and the Armenian Women's Rights Movement"
Martha Boudakian, State University of New York, Binghamton
"Giving Voice to Our Lives: The Politics of Identity"
Mariné Kurchian, Yerevan State University, Armenia
"The Distribution of Roles in the Family"

Chair: Joy Renjilian-Burgy, Wellesley College

Room 3   Claiming Legacies/Changing Lives: Toward an Armenian-American Feminist Theory
Arlene Voski Avakian, University of Massachusetts/Amherst
"Armenian-American Women's Self-Identification and Community Involvement"
Flora A. Keshgegian, Brown University, Providence, R. I.
"Orphaned Hope: The Legacy of Genocide and Armenian-American Women"
Janice Okoomian, Brown University, Providence, R. I.
"Gendered and Embodied Ethnicity in Carol Edgarian's Rise the Euphrates"
S. Shake Topalian, Psychotherapy Study Center, New York
"Victim to Survivor to Creating Our Own Lives: Armenian-American Women's Identities"
Chair: Arlene Voski Avakian, University of Massachusetts/Amherst

10:45 - 11:15 p.m.   Coffee Break
Bishop Partridge Hall

POLITICAL, CULTURAL, & SOCIAL EFFECTS OF INDEPENDENCE
11:15 - 1:00 p.m.   Plenary Session
Hoare Memorial Hall   Ludmila Harutunian, University of Yerevan, Armenia
"The Armenian Woman and Social/Political Innovations: Opportunities and Reality"
Gassia Apkarian, Armenian Assembly of America
"Women and Nation-Building"
Violetta Aghababian, Foreign Ministry, Armenia
"UNESCO's Role in Creating an Agenda for Armenian Women "
Nora Armani, actress, Paris, France
"Armenian Women in the Wake of Independence: A Documentary"

Jemma Ananian, Member of Parliament, Armenia
"Women and Local Government in Armenia"
Chair: Ludmila Harutunian, Yerevan State University

1:15 - 3:00 p.m.   *Luncheon*
Bishop Partridge Hall

Presentation of Woman of Achievement Awards

3-6 p.m.   *Bus Tour of London*

Wednesday, September 21, 1994

WOMEN AND HEALTH

9:00-10:45 a.m.   *Plenary Session*
Hoare Memorial Hall   Women's Health: An International View
Dr. Isabelle Valadian, Harvard School of Public Health
Dr. Marie Farrell, World Health Organization
Dr. Mary Khachikian, Ministry of Health, Armenia
Chair: Dr. Isabelle Valadian, Harvard School of Public Health

10:45-11:15   *Coffee Break*

11:15 a.m. - 1:00 p.m.   *Panel Sessions* (choose one of three)

Women's Reproductive Health
Judy Norsigian, Women's Health Book Collective
"Information is Power: The Armenian Armenian
Translation/Adaptation of The New Our Bodies, Ourselves"
Dr. Marine Sahakian, Women's Reproductive Health Center, Yerevan
"Women's Reproductive Health in Armenia"
Nora Nercessian, Harvard Medical School Alumni
"The Center for Women's Reproductive Health in Yerevan: An
Example in International Cooperation"
Chair: Alice K. Mirak, AIWA Vice-President

Effects of Environmental Pollution on Health: Assessment & Control
Gariné Danielian, Minister of the Environment, Armenia
"Women and the Environment"
Rita Aivazova, Director of Ecology, City of Yerevan
"The Role of Environmental Consciousness"
Aida Iskoyan, Yerevan State University, Armenia
"Protection of the Environment: Politics and Law"
Shakeh J. Kaftarian, Center for Substance Abuse Prevention
"Evaluation of Alcohol and Substance Abuse Among Women"
Chair: Eva Medzorian, AIWA Past President

Impact of Economic and Social Factors on Children
Vartiter Hovanissian, M.D., physician, Los Angeles
    "Overview of Health Concerns in Armenia and Karabagh"
Seda Kachatrian, pediatrician, Hospital #3, Yerevan
    "Armenian Infants: Nutritional Needs"
Octobrina Marutian, M.D., Maternity Hospital, Karabagh
    "Maternity Health Care in Time of War"
Araksi Kunderaciyan, Bergheim, Germany
    "Programs for Blind & Handicapped Children in Armenia"
Dr. Silva Karchikian, Los Angeles
    "How to Love, Protect, and Let Go"
Chair: Gina Hablanian, Digital Equipment Corp.

1:00 - 2:00 p.m.   *Luncheon*
Bishop Partridge Hall

2:15 - 4:15 p.m.   *Closing Plenary Session*
Hoare Memorial Hall   Recapitulation and Action Agenda
                            Gaining Power & Influence in Government and Business
                            The Armenian Heritage: Commitment and Change
                            Political, Cultural and Social Effects of Independence
                            Women and Health

                            Action Agenda Items

4:30 - 5:00 p.m.   *Afternoon Tea*
Bishop Partridge Hall

8:00 p.m.   *Independence Day Concert and Gala Reception*
Assembly Hall

AIWA Board of Directors, 1994-1995

Barbara J. Merguerian, *president*
Olga Proudian, *vice-president / special events*
Alice Mirak, *vice-president / directory*
Joy Renjilian-Burgy, *treasurer*
Geri Lyn Ajemian, *recording secretary*
Seta V. Nersessian, *corresponding secretary*
Sharyn S. Boornazian, *long-range planning*
Gina Ann Hablanian, *membership*
Doris D. Jafferian, *women of achievement*
Eva A. Medzorian, *human rights*
Agnes K. Missirian, *international liaison*
Natalie Zakarian, *programs / communications*
Rose Hovannesian, *ex officio, assistant treasurer*

AIWA Board of Directors, 1995-1996

Natalie Zakarian, *president*
Alice Mirak, *vice-president / bylaws*
Olga Proudian, *vice-president / special events*
Karen Bogosian, *vice-president / international liaison*
Karen Melikian, *recording secretary*
Joy Renjilian-Burgy, *corresponding secretary*
Ani Kharajian, *treasurer / international liaison*
Sharyn Boornazian, *long range planning / directory*
Doris Jafferian, *achievement awards*
Eva Medzorian, *republic of armenia liaison / special projects*
Barbara Merguerian, *information center and archives*
Suzanne Moranian, *membership*
Kristine Donabedian, *ex officio, legal consultant*
Rose Hovannesian, *ex officio, assistant treasurer*

London Conference Committee

Agnes K. Missirian, *Chair*
Annie Balikian
Joan Bamberger
Joyce Barsam
Gina A. Hablanian
Doris Jafferian
Cecile S. Keshishian
Eva A. Medzorian

Barbara Merguerian
Alice K. Mirak
Olga Proudian
Joy Renjilian-Burgy
Shushan Teager
Seta Terzian
Isabelle Valadian

West Coast Conference Committee

Elizabeth Agbabian
Candy Danielson
Tammy Dimitri
Flora Dunaians

Hermine Janoyan
Lilet Marzbetuny
Jasmine Mgrdichian
Savey Tufenkian

London Committee

Odette Bazil
Eileen Vartan Barker
Susan Pattie
Ani King-Underwood
Sossi Yeretsian

Janet Daghlian
Rosette Ouzounian
Tina Segel